The CHURCH of JESUS CHRIST on the MOVE

By
Archange Malonga

The Church of Jesus Christ on the Move

Authored and Published by Archange Malonga

Edited by Nathaniel Spiers of CharismaSolutions.org

Cover Design by Jerrold Daniels of DanielsDesignGroup.com

ISBN-13: 978-0692265734

ISBN-10: 0692265732

Prepared for print by Charisma Business Solutions www.CharismaSolutions.org

Unless otherwise stated all Scripture quotations come from the King James version of the Bible

www.ArchangeMalonga.com

www.ChurchOfJesusChristOnTheMove.com

CONTENTS

ACKNOWLEDGEMENTS

I want to thank my Lord and Savior Jesus Christ also I want to thank the Holy Spirit for His help and for leading me into all truth. I want to thank Yahweh (My Heavenly Father) the God of Abraham, Isaac, and Israel for trusting me with these messages. I count it all joy.

I want to thank my lovely wife and children for letting me have free time to write this book. I thank them for their sacrifices and the love they have towards me. I thank every man and women of God who has known me and has believed in me. I thank God for my Mom and Dad—for every investment they have made in my life.

I thank my sisters and brothers who prayed for me when I was under attack by the wicked one. I thank you all. I thank everyone who has sown their time when I needed them, and helped me publish this book, it was not easy but it's finally done. I love you all with the love of the Lord.

Drs. William and Veronica Winston, thank you for the good foundation that I have received for being under your leadership, it is because of the uncompromising Word of God you teach and preach, it has helped me grow and become a better son, husband, father and servant.

PREFACE

Every beginning of the year, I set aside time to seek the face and the mind of God for that year in prayer and fasting, I have been doing it for many years. I usually set a week apart to do that, but this year in 2014 I decided to seek God for 21 days, my agenda was to seek God about my life, my finances, my future, my children and family direction, it was all about me, little did I know, God had His own agenda in this fasting and prayer. Instead of telling me about me, He started to tell me about the church and His status. I was not thinking to write a book, but God made it clear that the church of Jesus Christ needs to be on the move.

Every day within the 21 days of praying and fasting, the Holy Spirit would reveal to me chapters to write and I was ready to write what He told me, I was in awe of the revelation that He was giving me on these topics. I could hardly contain myself sometimes because the presence was intense. There came times I could no longer share what I was witnessing because nobody could understand me when I tried to share with them what I was receiving as messages. And I was warned by the Spirit of God not to share anything with anyone until I finish the book, and I did just that until the time came to publish this book. It has been a joyful journey and I count it all joy that God would look upon me and trust me to write these topics that are dear to Him for the Body of Jesus Christ.

When I finished writing the book and I was ready to send it to the editor, the worse thing did happen, I lost the manuscript data on the computer and there was no trace of it anywhere, except on my iPhone, but the version I had on my iPhone was just the pre-introduction of what the chapter was about, I would say there were just snippets. When that happened I knew I was dealing with something special, I almost got upset but I knew it was a set up to steal my joy and block the connection I had with the Holy Spirit. It is impossible to explain how the data was lost, so I took 3 days off just praying and praising God. Then on the 4th day while everyone was sleeping I went back on the computer and rewrote the entire book all night within 24 hours. Now here is the finished product. I hope you enjoy reading this book as much as I enjoyed writing it, when the Holy Spirit gave me these subjects that cover the Mind of God over the church.

In case some of the places don't make sense to you, I just want to let you know that some of the messages on some of the chapters were discerned first in French and in my African dialects then were translated as simple as possible for the reader to understand, in case you misunderstand something I pray that the Holy spirit ministers to you in order to get what He meant when He gave me those revelations and messages.

CHAPTER ONE
GOD'S HAND IN THE CHAOS

⇄

The birth of every change start in chaos. God created the world in chaos (Genesis 1:1-24), He made man in chaos with mud (Genesis 1:26-29), and the world was dark when He spoke and there was light. The death of Jesus Christ on the cross was done in chaos, but the resurrection was the hand of God in the chaos. Never be afraid of chaos because God manifests Himself in the chaos.

"Mary, you are highly favored and you will carry the Son of God," "but I'm not married..." it sounded like chaos, but God had the plan that the Holy Spirit will be in the works to take care of that (Matthew 1:20-25).

King David went to fight Goliath with five stones and a sling shot when Goliath had spend all his life fighting and was skillful in all sorts of combat, but King David being a shepherd was no match for Goliath who, by the way, had a track record for never loosing a fight. It sounded like chaos—but in the chaos the hand of God was seen when a stone became more powerful than a sword (1 Samuel 17:40-52).

When God told Sarah that she will have a baby at 75 years old , it was shocking for her to hear since she has passed that stage of bearing; As a result of Abraham's faith in God, within the chaos the birth of Isaac was manifested (Genesis 18:10-12).

Another season of chaos took place in Abraham's life when God asked Abraham to sacrifice his son, Isaac. God saw Abraham's obedience in motion, replaced a lamb in Isaac's place. God gives us a preview in Abrahams life- The Lamb will be used for our salvation (Genesis 22:2-11).

People are complaining about the chaos in the world, yet every chaos has a purpose and a season.

> "But in the last days it shall come to pass, that the Lord shall be established in the top of the mountain, and it shall be exalted above the hills; and people shall flow into it. And many nations shall come, and say, come and let us go up to the mountain of the Lord, and the house of the God of Israel; and he will teach us of his ways, and we will walk in his paths: for the law shall go forth of Zion, and the word of the Lord from Jerusalem" (Micah 4:1-2)

The church is like an emergency room—it fix those who are broken, lost, and confused, giving them reassurance that everything will be better than ever before. We as the saints should witness to those that practice homosexual lifestyle, or those that live a promiscuous lifestyle, with love and truth of the Word of God. The heartbeat of God has to be the reflection of the church towards the lost souls. (Ephesians 2:19-20)

The question is: is the church ready to give them counsel without being judgmental and still be caring in the process? That's why this book is called *Church of Jesus Christ on the Move*, in order to move forward we need to see what God sees and feel what God feels toward His children and the church.

> "But in the last days it shall come to pass, that the Lord shall be established in the top of the mountain, and it shall be exalted above the hills; and people shall flow into it. And many nations shall come, and say, come and let us go up to the mountain of the Lord, and the house of the God of Israel; and he will teach us of his ways, and we will walk in his paths: for the law shall go forth of Zion, and the word of the Lord from Jerusalem" (Micah 4:1-2)

A big conversion of lost souls shall be added into the church, like it was in the book of Acts so shall be before the coming of Jesus Christ. If you are not willing to take your leadership seriously I'm sorry to tell you, but your position will be given to one who takes it more serious than you. God doesn't play when it comes to reaching out for souls.

Reuben's leadership was transferred to Joseph. Reuben was still considered as the elder, but his leadership was taken away from him, because he defiled his father bed (Genesis 49:3-4), he showed lack of leadership and he was demoted in his position as a leader of the family and Joseph was promoted. If you are not being responsible where God placed you and you are doing whatever, be careful your leadership can be given to whoever is responsible.

Saul's leadership was given to King David, the Bible said when King David was anointed by Prophet Samuel the Spirit of the Lord departed from Saul (1 Samuel 16:13-14). God can choose another to showcase His glory, stay humble and don't be moved by the chaos—because in the chaos the hand of God is seen.

CHAPTER TWO
TESTIMONY WILL CARRY YOU ON

⇄

Testimony is such a great word; this word has lost its importance amongst the saints. It has become a ritual and not a cherished word. God told the children of Israel to write down what He does for them so they can share it with their children and their children after them. You will see whenever the children of Israel had a challenge, they would repeat what God had done for their parents and God would act on their behalf after they repented and honored His Word. Gideon said, "Where are the miracles our fathers have told us..." (Judges 6:12-16). Psalms 78:2-72 talks about what God has done, the testimonies they carry with them of the Lord.

The testimony of the forefathers of Israel has helped them to remind God of what he did for them and what He promised them. A testimony is for your advantage and for the generation after you. You've got to have a testimony that your children and grandchildren can remember. It is for your benefit. It's easy to forget what God has done for you when all is going well, but when it is written, you can go back to it and see what God has done for you and fuel yourself with faith and assurance that God will come through for you whenever you face a challenge.

In Isaiah 43:26 God said, "bring me to remembrance and let's plead together..." Have a testimony book and share with your children how the Lord has brought you from where you were to where you are, and make a covenant with God that will be carried in your family for generations. God could not destroy Solomon when he changed his ways towards God because He remembered His covenant with King David (1 Kings 11:11-13). Let us not lose our ways but be the one who makes the difference.

Tell your children where your ministry started and what kind of obstacles you faced on your way to the top, how God delivered you, and how God promised you that your life and your ministry is in his hands. Have a testimony book.

Look what God told Moses about writing down testimonies: Exodus 17:14-15, "And the Lord said unto Moses, write this for a memorial in a book, and rehearse it in the ears of Joshua: for I will utterly put out the remembrance of Amalek from under heaven. And Moses built an altar, and called the name of it Jehovah-nissi." Exodus 34:27, "And the Lord said unto Moses, write you these words: for after the tenor of these words I have made a covenant with thee and with Israel.

When I read the Bible and see all those promises; I pray and ask God to give me my own promise, because some promises are personal and some are collective. And when He does—I write them down and I will share them with my children and their children after them. There is nothing greater than a personal Word for you and your family from God. Many times we try to hang on the promises of the forefathers in the Bible; they did obtain theirs, why don't you obtain your own? At the same time, don't forsake the promises they have obtained, because you will have to hang on some of their testimonies plus your own. Write down your testimonies it will carry you on.

CHAPTER THREE
LOVE FACTOR

⇄

Love is a choice as well as a commandment by God the Father. Love does not come as easy to some people even though it is an ultimate commandment we should walk and exercise every day.

1 John 2:8-12 says God is Love and Love is God—the God of Abraham, Isaac and Israel to be exact. He has shown us what Love is. I'm not talking about the one day event many people celebrate on February 14th of each year, but I'm talking about the lifestyle of Loving, Agape Love. Love without conditions. John 3:16 says, "God so Loved the world that he gave his only begotten Son, that whosoever believe in him shall never perish but have everlasting life."

When God sent his own Son Jesus Christ on the cross, it was not for His own interest, but for our interest, He gave His only begotten Son, so we would not perish. He gave the only precious thing He had for our sake. God will not allow you to perish because His Love never fails. If you perish it's because you are willing to perish. How can people perish? Through lack of knowledge and by not walking in Love. If you do not believe in Jesus Christ you are not walking in Love because He is the author of Love. The reason people don't walk in Love is because their relationship with Jesus Christ is not perfected.

"But God command his love toward us, because while we were yet sinners, Jesus Christ died for us ." (Romans 5:8)

"He died because he loves us. Every one that has his hope in him [Love] purifies himself. Even as he is pure." (1 John 3:3) Love cleanses our sins and weaknesses.

It's Love that defeated satan; satan knows that Love is a weapon. Jesus Christ hanging on the cross at Calvary was an act of Love. The reason Jesus Christ was persecuted on the way to the cross, is because the devil wanted Him to walk out of Love, but He remained silent and kept His Love walk for you and me, the sinners, and the ungodly. But Jesus Christ took all upon Himself because He Loves us. Love is the beginning of everything.

Love was in the beginning. God made Adam and Eve with Love. He could have stopped creating after creating the animals and kept all He had created to Himself, instead He went on and created Adam and Eve, me and you, and so forth. Love does not hold back what is right (1 John 3:11-19). Love is passionate; caring, patient, and wants the best for you and others—that is love.

Some people's blessings and answers to prayer are bound because of lack of Love. The scripture makes it clear in verse 22 and 23 of

1 John 3, that whatsoever we ask, we receive of Him, by keeping His commandment and 1 John 2:8-12 said love is a commandment. In verse 23 of 1 John 3 it says we should believe in Jesus Christ and Love one another. It is impossible to have the revelation of the Love of God and still walk in hatred. If you don't Love, you don't know God (1 John 4:7-21).

When you don't Love your brother or sister, you don't hate him or her, instead you hate Jesus Christ (John 15:18). We have known and believed the love that God has for us. "God is Love; and he that dwell in love is in God, and God in him," (1 John 4:16) and he goes on by saying,

> "Herein is our love made perfect, that we may have boldness in the day of judgment: because as He is, so are you in this world. There is no fear in love; but perfect love casts out fear: because fear has torment. He that fears is not made perfect in love. We love him, because he first loved us. If a man say; I love God, and hate his brother, he is a liar: for he that love not his brother whom he has seen, how can he love God whom he has not seen? And this commandment we have from Him, that he who Love God must love his brother also." (1 John 4:16-21)

Do not confuse abuse with love. When someone beats you and makes you look like you are not worth anything, messes up your face, makes you bleed, gives you a black eye, locks you in the house so you can't talk to anybody, that isn't love; that is abuse, control, and fear. You should stay away from such individuals because they can kill you because they are showing you how much they hate you and not love you. A husband who beats his wife, does it because his love is not perfected. You need to perfect your love towards yourself, because I have never seen anyone who Loves God and hates others.

I have heard a testimony of an ex-satanist, who used to be satan's top agent. He was saying that one day he came from a evil meeting and when he came back he could not get back in his body because a believer was praying in the building he was living in, and he said when a Christian prays every walls in that place become fire and that prevented him to re-enter his body because the walls were on fire and if he did try to enter he would have died on the spot so he decided to wait until she finished praying, but there was a problem, he was running out of time and was starting to get weak. Eventually was able to re-enter is body later on, but as a result he got really sick to the point of death because of that encounter.

So he was determined to avenge himself of that encounter, so he went to see his superiors in the evil camp and he told them about what happened to him and he told them that he will kill or hurt the person who almost killed him, and this is what the top agent of satan told him. You can't do anything about that woman, we have tried everything against her and nothing worked, but if you can get her upset and she does not walk in love: you can hurt or kill her in that moment. But we wish you the best because the woman is level 7+, 7+ that means she is high rank in the spirit and rank high in love. She was mature in the Word and the spiritual realm, understood satan tactics and knows who she is.

See, satan and his agents know that love is a weapon. Now if the woman was 5- or 7- he could have hurt her. If you are 1+ keep cultivating your love walk until you get to 5+ then why not a 7+ where that woman was. I pray that you keep your love walk and make peace with all those you have offended and forgive those who have offended you so satan does not have access to your joy, peace, and your blessing. You can get angry, but repent quick, so satan will not have you. Even the Bible says "be angry, and sin not: let not the sun go down upon your wrath" and verse 27 says, "neither give place to the devil" (Ephesians 4:26-27). Love is your shelter for protection and it is above everything.

CHAPTER FOUR
THE POWER OF VISION

⇄

Vision is a key factor in our lives, if you can't see where you are going—you will lose the purpose of being born. What I mean by that is that God created you for a reason and a great purpose and when you don't know your purpose it's easy to be irritated about life, while it shouldn't be the case based on the plan of God for your life. You are born and created for a purpose, your presence on earth is not random; it has a meaning. You are the world changer and the ambassador for the Kingdom of God (2 Corinthians 5:20). Many people are intimidated by the results other people get in life. The difference between that person and you is the mission and the vision. The Bible makes it very clear by saying "Without a vision people perish," (Proverbs 29:18). So people perish because of lack of vision.

God couldn't bless Abraham until his vision and mission was in line with God's plan for his life. He told him "As far as you can see," (Genesis 13:14-18 AMP). What you can see with your spiritual eyes is yours. If Abraham didn't see himself as the father of all nations (Genesis 17:4-6), God wouldn't have blessed him; because what you don't value, you will not have remorse giving away—but what you value, you protect with all might and cost.

Abraham drove away the birds that came down to eat the offering he prepared before God. In other words, the birds wanted to steal his promise and blessing so he drove them away so he could be blessed. Because he did that, God revealed to him the vision for his blood line (Genesis 15:9-14). Abraham valued the offering, therefore he protected it at any cost—that is the power of the vision he carried in him. Jacob couldn't have multiply the livestock which he had when he was working with his uncle, if he had no vision for the future (Genesis 30:31-43). You can tell how big a person's vision is based on how you carry yourself and act.

A visionary is responsible, very organized, and focused to achieve the vision they carry. The manifestation of your vision doesn't depend on your critics but it depends on you. When you are a visionary you will not participate in things that will rob you of your destiny. Not corruption, not bribery, not sexual temptation, those things will come, but stay away from them, it will cost you more than the deception that comes with it. It may sound good to do those things but they end up destroying your destiny; it's deception. It's satanic, satan made it sound good by telling Eve if she eats the fruit she will be like God (Genesis 3:4), and the Bible said Eve was deceived (1 Timothy 2:14), deception always robs you from your destiny and it always tends to sound good.

Examine the situation and never rush. There is a saying in real estate that says, anything that is verbal can be considered as a written agreement, get it in writing to cover yourself. You need to know this there is no secret, be careful who surround yourself with because your surrounding can short cut your destiny for anything done in darkness will be revealed by the light. (Ephesians 5:13). The light is when God is protecting you because of your integrity and the darkness is where the devil is throwing you a bait to tarnish your image through bribery, lies, and evil report. You are what you do in secret when no one is looking. It's not for nothing God said He sees what you do in secret and He will reward you openly (Matthew 6:6). Why is that? Because God knows your secret life.

CHAPTER FIVE
FRIEND OF GOD

$$\rightleftarrows$$

The growth of your faith is connected to what you hear and are exposed to. The children of Israel cried over the evil report the spies brought back and it caused them to fear for their lives. But it took Joshua and Caleb to lead them to the promise land, you don't need a lot to build your faith, Joshua and Caleb are two against ten, but the two were more powerful than the ten. When you team up with God, you become the majority. Joshua and Caleb did not let the circumstances dictate their faith in God; instead they let their faith in the Word of God dictate the situation for them. "If there is two or three gathered in my name, there I am in their midst" (Matthew 18:20) the power of agreement, because they agreed to believe and trust God, God was with them.

I will rather be confident that God is with me than being confident people are with me. People can change their minds, but God can't, because, "Forever His Word is settle in Heaven," (Psalms 119:89). What He said, He will do, because God can't lie. (Numbers 23:19). Abraham believed God and he was called the friend of

God. His faith caused God to call him His friend. Now Abraham and God do not have the same age, if you view it that way, but because of his faith in God, God called him His friend (James 2:23). So regardless your age; when you walk by faith God will call you His friend. Build up your faith and take God at His Word regardless of the situation or how many years you will have to wait for the promise to manifest. As long as you know that God is with you and the promise is His, stay put because He will bring it to pass because of your faith in Him.

If you want to please God, be a person of faith. "Without faith it is impossible to please God," (Hebrews 11:6).

Faith comes by hearing and hearing by the Word of God (Romans 10:17). What you hear can either build your faith or bring doubt into your life. If you set your ears to unbelief, sooner or later doubt will rule your life. Doubt will kill you, but faith will save you.

CHAPTER SIX
THE WORD

⇄

"Now the parable is this: The seed is the Word of God. Those by the way side are they that hear; then come the devil, and take away the word out of their hearts, lest they should believe and be saved." (Luke 8:11-12).

You become what you speak and what you believe becomes what you expect. God can't and will not do anything without his Word because: "In the beginning was the Word and the Word was with God," (John 1:1-3). Whatever God does the Word has to be the first step. From creation God as always used the Word as the cornerstone of His work, just as it was in the beginning when He said let there be light (Genesis 1:3), not only that, "The words you speak they are spirit and they are life." (John 6:63). The Word of God is seed (Luke 8:11) and like any other words they are seeds as well, because, "Life and death is in the power of the tongue," (Proverbs 18:21), life and death is in the words you speak out of your mouth, the power of spoken word and confession.

"How can two walk together unless they agree," (Amos 3:3), in order to become like God you will have to agree with His Word also you will have to be willing with your mind (Philemon 1:14) Also God said in Psalm 138:2 that He will exalt His Word above His Name, His word guarantees you to prevail over anything when used in faith. His Word will not return to you void (Isaiah 55:11); in other words His word can't return without proof. There is power in the Word of God. Whenever you use it, He said you should see evidence, that the Word have power.

Do not restrain the Word of God through unbelief, for the Word of God does good to him that walk uprightly (Micah 2:7) and Psalm 45:1 says your tongue edits the matter, satan can't curse you, when the curse is issued you have to use your tongue to cancel it, nobody can curse whom God has blessed (Numbers 23:8). Why is that? Because when the curse is issued, your tongue has the power to cancel it with the Word of God found in the scriptures. Psalm 64:1-10 talks about arrows that are sent to afflict the children of God, these contentions are works of witchcraft. How do they issue them? Through evil pronunciation against the individual, but your tongue can veto anything that the devil target towards you, you are not what the devil said you are, but you are what God says you are. Proverbs 12:18 says the wise speak health, you don't confess sickness over you when you feel something or when diagnosed with something, you speak the Word of God over you, confess health over you, veto sickness, and decree by the stripes of Jesus Christ you were healed (Isaiah 53:5).

God said I will not allow any sickness on you that is on the heathen, (Deuteronomy 7:15) this is a written and spoken promise by God, and we have to believe and stand on these promises given to us. By His stripes you were healed, you were, so you are already healed by the stripes He suffered on the cross for you. Why would you pay a debt that was already paid for you by our Savior? He is the Lord that heals you (Exodus 15:26). When a debt is paid and you try to challenge it, the court usually request proof that shows if the debt was paid in full, well I got news for you, your proof is the Word of God, Jesus Christ said it is finished (John 19:30). Nobody can accuse you or con you unless you allow it. James 3:5-6 says the tongue is so little when you look at it, but when not used properly it causes big damage, when you use the Word of God properly against satan; it creates damage in the kingdom of darkness.

We see it in the media outlets, someone makes a comment and the next thing all his contracts are cancelled and so forth, because it is the evidence of the words we speak can do. So choose your words carefully. James 4:7-10 says resist the devil and he will flee from you, see, it takes resistance to make the devil run from you. When you stick with the Word, you grow more in God and the devil has no choice but to flee. So when you are tempted and afflicted your first resort is the Word of God, that is the only way you can chase out satan.

When Jesus Christ was tempted by satan His first resort was the Word of God by saying, "it is written," anytime he tried towards Jesus Christ, His reply was "It is written," He told satan what the

Word of God said about the situation he wanted to tempt Jesus Christ with. If you are tempted to fornicate you should say:

"Fornication is a sin and my body is the temple of God (1 Corinthians 6:19) also it says in 1 Thessalonians 4:3-4, For this the will of God, even your sanctification, that you should abstain from fornication: that everyone of you should know how to possess his vessel in sanctification and honor." The Bible encourages not to live by bread alone but by every Word of God that proceed out of your mouth (Luke 4:4). James 4:17 says therefore to him that know how to do good and do it not, to him it is sin."

Encourage yourself in The Lord (1 Samuel 30:6) by using the Word of God when things don't go your way, or when people criticize you.

Asa trusted in everyone except God and God let him die. He went to the physicians and everybody else except God (2 Chronicles 16:7-12).

The seer came to guide him in the right direction, now he is mad at the wrong person, someone who is trying to lead him in the right path and he is refusing to take instruction and to repent from his wrong doing. The Bible says, "Touch not my anointed and do my prophets no harm. He put the seer in jail for telling him the truth. How many people do we know, who get mad at the pastor (the prophet) for correcting them? He should have been mad at the devil for misleading him and not at the prophet. All he is doing is following instructions given to him because God doesn't want to see a sheep perish. By the way, the Word of God is for reproof and for correction (2 Timothy 3:16-17), don't challenge the quality of the Word that comes your way, but welcome it and use it to change.

A pastor shall not always tell you what makes you comfortable, whenever you are out of line, he has to correct you based on the Word of God and the leading of the Spirit of God. Many people love people who sponsor their foolishness. The person who tells you the truth is the person who loves you, even God chastise whom He loves (Revelation 3:19), you may not care about yourself, but when someone who cares come to you, be thankful because not many people get that opportunity, use your words wisely, for words have power.

CHAPTER SEVEN
HELL IS REAL, SO IS HEAVEN

$$\rightleftarrows$$

Many people debate if hell is real, I have good news for you, hell is real and it is not a lie.Here is an encounter where Jesus Christ is telling us about a man who went to hell: The rich man ended up in hell and was tormented while Lazarus the beggar ended up in Heaven in Abraham's bosom (Luke 16:20-25). Those who qualify will be in Heaven (Luke 10:20)

I have a question for you, if you can answer it then you have the answer whether hell is real or not. Do you believe God exists? If your answer is yes, then you are right. Do you believe satan exists? If you believe that, you are right as well. Satan is the god of hell. That's where those who don't work their salvation with fear and trembling will end up (Philippians 2:12) Jesus Christ Himself went to hell to destroy what satan has stolen from God (Colossians 2:14-15) The Bible said He spent 3 days in hell and stripped satan of his title as the god of this world. Look what the Bible does not say, Jesus Christ did not stay there, He just went to hell to take back what satan had stolen, so if you are not in Jesus Christ when you die you will go to hell and stay there, only those who are in Jesus Christ will go to Heaven where Jesus Christ is. Revelation 21:8 talks about hell as well.

This topic is not talked about as much, and many people have gone to hell because of that. Psalms 90:12 says to, "Teach us to number our days, so we may apply our hearts to wisdom." In everything there is a second way, you can be poor and become rich, you can be sad and become joyful, you can be sick and become whole, you can be single and be married or re-married, but when you die you can't come back to make a decision about what you want to do with your life or where you want to end up when you die, it's over at that point. You end up where you end up and nothing can be done about it, that's how it is.

God loves you so much but He will not violate His Word because you refuse to obey when you had the opportunity to do so. I love the way Evangelist Billy Graham ministers, when he is closing on his message, he always reminded people of Heaven and hell and opened the floor for the altar call, when people understood what was at stake and analyzed their lives they came to give their lives to Jesus Christ without a problem.

Today the altar call is often rushed, not many churches take this seriously, some churches don't even have altar calls, the altar call is the most important part of the service, the wall between hell and Heaven, who knows after you step out of that church what will happen to you, many times death comes without a warning, and that moment should not be taken lightly. At least three times a year this message of Heaven, hell, and repentance needs to be taught over and over again, the message of prosperity is good but it's not the greatest message, the greatest message is the winning of souls that's what touches God the most, money can be restored, anything in life can be restored but when a soul dies without Jesus Christ there is no restoration at that point.

I remember when we had a men's fellowship at my church after the man of God open the floor for the altar call, I thank God for my man of God and his persistence when it comes to souls, he was closing the service and he ran out of time and cared less about time at that moment because of the witness he felt from the Holy Spirit and he stretched out by saying there is somebody out there you need to come and give your life to Jesus Christ; and he said I'm not closing until you come; guess what the person came and gave his life to Jesus Christ and got baptized in the name of Jesus Christ, and received the baptism of the Holy Spirit with evidence of speaking in tongues; a few days later he got into an accident, he was a truck driver, and his truck flipped over and he died. If the man of God did not make this his priority this man would have ended in hell.

Today people live any way, man with man, woman with woman, living in the same house and not married, married but have a partner on the side, stealing from the church, sleeping with the members of your church, going to night clubs, that aches God's heart if you are not living a life of repentance and holiness you are walking on a thin line, let's not take God's grace for granted, there comes a time the grace of God can't be extended to you, after death there is no extension of grace. People are more afraid of death than of the sin, while you should fear sin more than death, because the wages of sin is death (Romans 6:23). When I see people go to night clubs and they show off their cars, money, and clothes; women flock at them and they feel powerful, it hurts me because if they can see what is at stake in case something goes wrong during that time. Let me tell you something, that wouldn't be good after all that show off, when death strikes all that fun become a burning fire, work on your salvation and stay close to God. Hell is real indeed.

I give you an example, parents can teach and do whatever they want for their child, but if the child goes out there and does something silly, and there is proof the child did it, now the decision is in the court of law to decide and follow the law in place, at that time the Parents are helpless because the law needs to be followed all they can do is cry as their child is taken away. Well it's the same when we are not following what God said and satan comes and find fault. And the blood of Jesus Christ was not applied because you did not repent, God can't do anything about it because there is no proof of your confession to God that you did repent, he has to let you go to satan, it pains God to see that happen, but he has to follow the law in place, the wages of sin is death but in Jesus Christ you have eternal life, forgiveness of sins and so forth (Romans 6:23). This message is so real, because Jesus Christ spent a good time of his ministry pointing people to Heaven and the life of repentance. When you live this life style, you don't have to work so hard for the blessing because Heaven is open above you and it will answer you before you even call (Isaiah 65:23-24).

When I see the funeral of a gang banger and they come out with T-shirts that says rest in peace, I cry, and I demand God to open their eyes. What makes you think he is at peace? Did he receive Jesus Christ as his Savior when he was on earth how much wrong he did, did he repent of what he has done, when you live a life of repentance you can't remain the same, so I doubt he repented otherwise he would have left the gang, did he repent before he got shot and if he did not repent, he is going to hell no doubt about it, and the pastor that does the funeral does not talk to them about this, and after the funeral it's business as usual.

You have to tell people the truth and let them know what is at stake. That should be a time to win souls since you can't go to them now they came up to you, it should be time to showcase the goodness of your God and not be afraid of them. Satan is really wicked, the gang is a product of hate and disobedience, you want to make your own rules and live your own life, the Word of God says the law is not made for the righteous man, but for the lawless and disobedient, for the ungodly (1 Timothy 1:9) while the Bible says obey those who are in authority.

Many are in hell because they failed to change and work on their salvation, (Philippians 2:12) Though it may seem so now, tattoos on your body is not a sign of toughness, what makes you tough is believing in Jesus Christ, because in Him you overcome every battles. If you fail to change and you happen to go to hell, you become tormented and no one can help you there (Luke 16:22-24) that is a terrible thing. In verse 28 of Luke 16 the rich man tells them he has five brothers and he wishes the gospel can be preached to them so they don't come where he is—in the place of torment. In my Bible it is in red which means it's Jesus Christ talking, He is reminding us of the encounter of this rich man, he had money, honors, servants, and titles, but upon death without Jesus Christ all those things meant nothing, he was tormented and not at peace. He was in hell, a place of no return after death without Jesus Christ.

There is a topic that rose up about if a Christian or someone committed suicide, would they go to Heaven or hell? This is a topic that requires honesty by answering to those who want to hear it. You did not create yourself, God created you indeed for a purpose and a mission, in Jeremiah God said, "Before I formed you in your mother's womb, I knew you and ordained you a prophet to the nations." (Jeremiah 1:4-5), everyone is ordained by God to do something for His glory. Why don't you go to Him since He ordained and formed you so He can tell you what is going on and what you need to focus on? you can't end your life because of challenges in life, people tend to stand on this scripture where sin abound more, grace abound much more (Romans 5:20) not so my friend, when sin abounds grace abounds much more, just like in the times of Noah, people were living in sin the grace was extended to them to repent, but they did not and when the flood came they were all destroyed, so the grace abound is when God is giving you time to get your life together and seek Him and not to end it.

It's a tragedy to witness such a thing, it's painful to talk about it, but you have to talk about it so we don't lose more people to satan because of ignorance (2 Corinthians 2:11) I feel for those parents who have served God and their child committed suicide on their watch, we need to talk about this with our loved ones, they need to know that a blessing can be transferable but salvation is a personal matter, I can't transfer my salvation to my children, they have to work their own, I can pass down my blessing to my children, Abraham passed on his blessing to Isaac and Israel (Genesis 28:4-5).

If you are Abraham's seed, then heir according to the promise (Galatians 3:29) many people of God don't share with their love ones that hell is real and to live a life of repentance and to be serious with God. No one will go before God with an excuse, everybody in life will get opportunities to hear the message of salvation and repentance before they die so they can be spared from hell, the key is, will you listen and take it seriously, as the Bible said, "today if you hear his voice harden not your hearts, as in the provocation, in the day of temptation in the wilderness," (Hebrews 3:7-8).

I have heard testimonies of people who God took to hell and brought them back on earth to warn us of the danger that is before us, the thing they always expand on is hell is real and they saw loved ones and they are telling them to run from hell and go tell others to avoid that place, these are real testimonies, it's not there to scare you but to warn you. It sounds like in (Luke 16:28) and

God is saying let's live a life of repentance even though grace is there to carry us to Heaven.

Prayer of Repentance Against Suicide Thoughts

Heavenly Father, the God of Abraham, Isaac and Israel.

I ask you for forgiveness for thinking and trying to commit suicide, Yahweh help me get rid of such thoughts and give me positive thoughts.

God you have created me for a purpose, I pray that you guide me and reveal to me my purpose which you have created me for. I ask for Strength in times of weakness when I feel alone and unworthy. My God, I remit my destiny and my life into your hands and I know you see my end before I can reach it. I depend on you and I put my trust in you.

Holy Spirit; help me in this walk until my time comes to be called in the presence of God. In the name of Jesus Christ I ask and receive the freedom of living my life according to your plan.

In Jesus Christ of Nazareth I pray. Amen

Personal testimony

Let me give you my testimony, a few years ago; I was so tired of being alive and dealing with a lot of problems. I have heard many times when you die; you will not have any more problems? That's partially true, but it depends where you end up. Heaven is the only place where there are no problems at all. I came to realize that later on. I thought it was a good illusion, it's better to die than live so I don't have any more problems.

I thank God I was saved then and I could hear the voice of God. I wanted to start a business and I had no money, no support from family and I had no friends which could see where I was going. So I came up with a good idea (at least I thought) and my last resort plan, I went to see one of my relative who had some money and I asked him, if I die today how much would it cost to ship my body from America to Africa, I was single then and young. He said it will cost around $20 thousand.

I was in shock when I heard it; that was a lot of money to me. So I told him, why don't you give me that money, I have an idea to start a business and that money will help me a lot, if I die and I didn't use that money wisely, give my body to the state and let them bury me "I sound very desperate here" that's how determined and deceived I was at the same time. It's God who supplies all your need and not your relatives (Philippians 4:19) I came to understand that later on, to make a long story short.

He refused to agree with me, so I wrote a letter and highlighted what I wanted to accomplish, God does inspire me with worship songs and messages to His glory and so forth, and I wanted to start a gospel recording label, and that money would have helped me launch the business as I inquire extra on a loan from the bank. And in the letter I said please continue this work for me, open this recording label and a portion of every profit you make, give it to this church to finance the gospel and the rest use it for this and that, it sounded good but not to God. Then after that I was going to commit suicide, when I was ready to do it, I heard a clear voice said, if you do it you are going to hell and I can't do nothing about it. It was not an audible voice, yet it was so clear and peaceful.

I stopped what I was trying to do at that moment; that voice changed my life forever. See, nobody can do what God has assigned you to do, I have been given instruction how to go about the mission God has placed in my heart, how to start this company, but no one could do what I was called to do.

You need to realize that you are unique and nobody can replace you, no one matches your finger print, or your iris that's how unique you are. There are not two like you, you are a limited edition. We spend more when our love one dies; we buy an expensive head stone, T-shirts, and other things, but we don't invest in them when they are alive. It should be the opposite, invest in them to live the life that is pleasing to God instead of waiting until they die. When was the last time you have prayed and fasted for your love one, when was the last time you had a discussion about hell and Heaven with your loved ones, when was the last time you asked to pray with them, when was the last time you invited them to church while you are interceding for God to touch them as they come. But when death strikes we are surprised and we feel regret for not doing more before the end. There is a man in South America who said when he dies he wants his Bentley to go with him in his tomb. What a deception. When he goes to Heaven or hell he can't enjoy it, if he goes to Heaven he can't enter with it because Heaven has everything, and if he goes to hell someone will take it away from him.

I heard a Man of God share this testimony: A man died and wanted to take gold with him to Heaven. As he arrived at the gate, the angel told him he can't enter with it into Heaven and he said, "Why not," the angel replied, "Heaven doesn't need it, there is plenty of gold here, the streets are path with gold, we don't need your crumbs." What I'm trying to say here is, your salvation will guarantee you a peaceful and abundant life when you are focused on Jesus Christ and live a life that pleases him.

The wages of sin his death, but Jesus Christ guarantee eternal life. Don't believe in purgatory when you die, it is a deception and it does not exist, it's a deception from the pit of hell, nobody can pray you out of hell once you have expired, it doesn't matter how long people fast for you, it doesn't matter how many masses are done on your behalf—it's a nice thought—but God will not show mercy and forgive their sins because of your yearnings, they will not come back and you are not paving a path to heaven for them either through your prayers and masses. It is what it is. I wonder about those who are telling you purgatory exist. I ask if they have read the Bible or do they really care about the well being of your life, because they are not leading you to God but to satan.

I wish people will read the Bible and books that edify for their own enrichment instead of believing what the man said because of tradition and not revelation. False information is causing many people to miss entering Heaven, do your own homework, you are the captain of your soul and destiny. This is serious, don't leave it in the hands of someone else to manage it for you. Many ways lead to God, but there's only one path that leads to Heaven it's through Jesus Christ of Nazareth and not anyone else. Take your life seriously and keep building up your relationship with God.

Death is never the end of your life; it's the beginning of where you will spend the rest of your life. It's either Heaven or hell.

One of the biggest mistakes many people make is that they become so comfortable with God and the things of God. Never become comfortable, because you will be prone to not yield to the revelation behind the truth that is being revealed to you, which will set you free. The Bible said Joseph told his brothers and father about his dreams, but there is a particular dream he told him, the Bible said Israel observe the saying. (Genesis 37:9-10) In other words, he wanted to know more and see the manifestation of it, he didn't ignore it. There came a time when the dream came to pass of what God revealed about his plan for Joseph and his family (Genesis 42:9). Didn't Joseph rule over his brothers like the dream said, yes he did. This shows you whatever God said it will come to pass, hell and Heaven is mentioned in the Bible therefore it does exist. The virgin Mary will not lead you to Heaven, if your faith is in the virgin Mary to pray for you to Jesus Christ so you can go to Heaven, you are being deceived, she is just like you and me, pray to Jesus Christ and not Mary. Acts 4:12 says, "Neither is there Salvation in any other: for there is none other name under heaven given among men, whereby we must be saved," and that name is Jesus Christ and not Mary.

CHAPTER EIGHT
BELIEVE GOD AT HIS WORD

⇄

"And it came to pass as the Man of God had spoken to the King, saying, two measures of barley for a shekel, and a measure of fine flour for a shekel, shall be tomorrow about this time in the gate of Samaria:

"And the Lord answered the man of God, and said, now, behold, if the Lord should make windows in heaven, it might such a thing be? And he said, behold, you shall see it with your eyes, but shall not eat thereof.

"And so it fell into him: for the people trode upon him in the gate, and he died." (2 Kings 7:18-20)

When God tells you something, do not argue with Him. He has more wisdom than you. Believe Him and take note to what He has told you. God is a better counselor you can depend on…

He is the key to your existence. Why dare question Him when you know that it is Him talking to you? If you have doubt, ask Him if it's Him, but don't doubt when you know it's Him. Peter had this revelation when he came against the wind while on the boat (Matthew 14:26-31); he said, "Jesus Christ is that you? If it's you allow me to come;" and Jesus Christ told Him come and he came. He heard Jesus Christ well, his sinking on water was not that he did not hear, nor was it doubt if he heard well, it was lack of assurance that caused him to sink because of the sound of the wind.

It could be something he experienced before at sea or a story he was told when he was a child about how somebody vanished at sea when there was the wind—we don't really know the scope of why he changed his focus when he had engaged his faith and knew his decision was not natural. For some reason he changed the course of his focus away from His Savior.

What is causing you to lose focus? What wind is in your life when God has told you to meet Him? Just like Jesus Christ told Peter "Fear not, you will not sink, just believe and don't doubt!" Whatever you need in life, as long you have the Word from God you are on the right path, the Word of God abides forever (1 Peter 1:23) Everything will pass away but God's word will always remain. (Luke 24:35) Your freedom is connected in believing God's Word.

CHAPTER NINE
ARE YOU INFLUENCED BY THE WORD OR THE WORLD

⇄

"And be not conformed to this world: but be ye transformed by the renewing of your mind, that you may prove what is good, and acceptable, and perfect, will of God" (Romans 12:2)

The church has become so comfortable with the result it has obtained from many, many years; and at some point the church has neglected to evaluate the direction it is going. Few churches have caught the revelation of transforming the believers under the sound of their leader by teaching the right doctrine without compromise, but many churches are not faced by any form of transformation. They continue to transact business as usual, without evaluating the advancement of the mandate given: To evangelize, teach, reach, seek and save which is lost. We have big conferences and many times it's for a show for those who attend or a ritual as an act of presence but not a time of encounter and transformation. Only those who are serious with God leave a conference transformed and renewed.

We become so in love with slogans and are not being glued to the transformation of the Word of God. God wants us to be transformed to the glory of the Kingdom and His Name. It takes willingness and dedication in order to be transformed, your act of presence is not going to transform you, but your yearning and dedication will. Peter was transformed, he was willing and yearning for transformation, he used to curse now he is saying, "Silver and gold I have not but in the name of Jesus Christ rise up and walk." (Acts 3:6-7) He is in the healing business now, he is a transformed person. Mary Magdalene used to be a prostitute but now she is announcing the good news, He is risen, Jesus Christ is risen, she was transformed by the gospel (John 20:11-18). God is interested in transformation and not in slogans.

Transformation makes impact. Slogans excite for a moment, but die quickly because it was done in enthusiasm and not out of impartation. Transformation takes place when it touches the soul, the mind, and the spirit and it becomes imprinted in you and your eyes are open for deeper revelation. We need transformation in the church. We need to be more engaged in the depth of the Word with God being the center of the outcome we expect. The more you read the Word of God, the deeper revelation you get into, because the Word is for our benefit and growth. You are as transformed as the revelation you carry. But you are un-transformed by the information you miss-carry.

The church is not the place to hand you over into the hands of satan, instead the church is the central place that leads you into the plan of God for eternity. That is the whole essence of the church: to preserve you until the coming of Jesus Christ. Your whole life ought to be the reflection of the DNA that you carry of God, not the reflection of satan. The Word of God ought to influence your life and not the deceiving ways of the world. If it's not in the Word of God, don't approve of it, because it will destroy you and prevent you from being a transformed believer.

CHAPTER TEN
WHO ARE YOU?

⇄

Are you a professing Christian or are you a cheerleader Christian? A professing Christian displays fruit; but a cheerleader Christian is a Christian that cheer others, yet is not willing to put in effort to bear fruit.

Most people in the church are influenced by the world and not by the Word. They listen to worldly music (secular music) that insult our daughters and tarnish the image of our sons, full of profanity and so forth. Church people sponsor the secular lifestyle more than they sponsor gospel music or lifestyle, people go to church but their mind is not transformed, you can tell a transformed person by their decisions and actions.

Apostle Paul was transformed when Jesus Christ became his Lord and Savior, he stopped killing people and he started saving souls. People go to church but still spend overnight in the clubs and strip clubs like they have never been saved. The world dictates what they shall become and not the Word. They believe more what the world says than what the Word says. They honor the idols more than their pastor, apostle and prophet. I didn't say worship them, I said honor them.

Wherever you go, are you mindful of the church you attend? Do you know that any foolish decision you make reflects on the church you attend? Your pastor should be the reflection of what you are taught, if you are known as a women user it reflects on the church you attend, when you are a drug dealer it reflects on the church you attend, if you are a pimp or a prostitute it reflects on the church you attend and your pastor, you become what you eat and what you believe.

The church is supposed to put those venues out of business. Secular musicians make more money than gospel artists and they are not the ones who sponsor the gospel but hates it, and those who are supposed to bring their tithes are not doing so. Why is that? because they are not transformed—because the Saints won't support their own, this is the honest truth—if there is a secular artist having a concert few blocks away from a gospel artist, many church goers will flock to see the secular artist, why?Because they love the world more than the Word; while the Word of God says when you are friend with the world you become God's enemy. (James 4:1-8) You are in the world but not of the world (John 17:16) stop being a cheerleader and be a professing and believing Christian.

CHAPTER ELEVEN
THE POWER OF FORGIVENESS

⇄

"And when you stand praying, forgive, if you have ought against any: that your Father [God] also which is in heaven may forgive you your trespasses. But if you do not forgive, neither will your Father [God] which is in heaven forgive your trespasses" (Mark 11:25-26).

Forgiveness is a taboo subject, it's not something new at all; it has been talked about for many, many centuries, it was the core message of greats such as Martin Luther King, Mother Theresa, Gandhi and so forth. It's a decision that requires you to lower yourself and still feel big on the inside, a lifestyle that requires strength that no one can give but only through God's grace. Forgiveness is not easy for some because they don't understand the power that comes with forgiveness. Even God himself had to go through that, Jesus Christ cried on the cross because of our sins saying, "Father forgive them because they know not what they do," (Luke 23:34). Can you imagine how Jesus Christ felt, He was beaten for our sake and still He is saying, "Father forgive them, for they know not what they do." That is big on His part, He didn't have to do that, but He is leading by example, His cry didn't take away the God out of Him, it made Him even bigger. Forgiveness is not an occasional act; it is a constant attitude and lifestyle.

We have to be loving and caring; because when you look at the sacrifice of the cross as it says in scripture, "When we were yet sinners Jesus Christ died for us." (Romans 5:8)

The Bible stretches this further, "How can you love God whom you have not seen but can't love your brother or sister whom you see?" (1 John 4:20) in other words, how can you love God and hate your brother and sister, don't you know that the love you have for God is connected with your brother and sister.

Jesus Christ said, "If you forgive men their trespasses, your Heavenly Father will also forgive you: but if you forgive not men their trespass, neither will your Father forgive your trespasses." (Matthew 6:14-15) And He was telling His disciples about it. How to pray and forgiveness was extended in that discussion because it is a must in the life of a believer (Matthew 6:9-15). Do not let your prayer become noise before God because you are not willing to forgive in your heart (Matthew 6:6-7). Your answered prayer is connected in your forgiveness, healing, harvest, and blessing—all of those—are connected to the degree you are willing to forgive.

Example

One day, when my son was three years old, I happened to make hot chocolate milk and I told him to stay out of the kitchen because I had hot milk in there. He asked me if I could give him some, I said no, because it was hot at the moment, also his supper was almost ready and I didn't want him to lose his appetite.

I happened to make a quick trip in the bedroom and I heard noise that sounded familiar then I came out, guess who was that, my son with his clothes wet and a mustache, I spanked him because he could have burned himself, he went to his Mom crying, trying to see if she will side with him and she didn't, then he cried louder to no result then he came back to me to apologize and my response was cold, he said I'm sorry Daddy and I told him I don't want to hear that, not in a good way at all. I wanted him to feel how upset I was with him, since my response was cold, he turned away and cried some more, then the Holy Spirit spoke to me, He said to me when I make a mistake and come to God for forgiveness does God tells me He doesn't want to hear it? Once He said that I ran to my son who was sitting next to his Mom and I told him sorry, that I do forgive him, and I gave him a hug.

See, when someone hurts you, it takes a lot to forgive, but remember God forgives you every time you mess up, since God does it to you, why can't you do that to someone else? Forgiveness is not a choice but a must. When you don't forgive you are the one hurting and not the other person, I guaranty you the other person may have moved on and doesn't think about the issue anymore, or even they forgot all about it altogether, and you are there hurting yourself because you don't want to forgive.

If Nelson Mandela did not forgive, he wouldn't have left South Africa in good shape, people would have been divided and chaos would have invaded that country, but because of forgiveness, peace reigned in that country and on the people. Jesus Christ died on the cross for you and forgave you, why can't you forgive someone else —even yourself. Learn to forgive so you don't miss out on your blessing.

CHAPTER TWELVE
REPENTANCE

⇄

"I came not to call the righteous, but sinners to repentance" (Luke 5:32)

"Repent you: for the Kingdom of Heaven is at hand." (Matthew 3:2)

Repentance is the way to keep in touch with our God. Everybody wants to go to Heaven, but no one is willing to die. Everyone wants to be blessed, but no one is willing to repent. The life of repentance glorifies God; it shows that you are walking in His fear and in His love.

The Bible says, "Repent and be baptized... and you shall receive the gift of the Holy Ghost." (Acts 2:38) Also it says if you have an argument with you brother and you bring a gift to God, the Bible said go make it good with your brother then come back (Matthew 5:23-24). See, Heaven does not answer you when you can't live a life of repentance, even before the gift of the Holy Spirit comes to you; you need to repent. The Scripture said, "Repent, and be baptized every one of you in the name of Jesus Christ for the remission of sins, and you shall receive the gift of the Holy Spirit." (Acts 2:38) This should tell you something: that sin can block the answer to your prayer. "Husband love your wife so your prayer be not hindered," (1 Peter 3:7) These are simple requests given to us, but they carry powerful effect when you ignore them.

Today many people blame God for not answering them, the question is, have you checked yourself before you accuse God? When you sowed your seed, was it sown in love or in quarrel with someone during that time? Are you holding grudges in your heart so you feel like you could never let it go? The Bible says, "Guard your heart with all diligence for out of it comes the issues of life." (Proverbs 4:23) People will always offend you, people will betray you, Judas Iscariot betrayed Jesus Christ with a kiss and money (Matthew 26:47-48) but Jesus Christ had to forgive him.

Repentance is key in your relationship with God, repentance does not take away anything from you instead it adds more to you. King David was called a man after God's own heart, yet he was a killer; he killed the woman's husband so he can be with her. (2 Samuel 11:14-17) This is a crime worthy of a death sentence, yet the Bible calls him a man after God's own heart. Why is that? Because King David knew how to live a life of repentance; he repented when he blew it, and God loved him for that.

Repentance keeps your spiritual pipe open, so you can hear God clearly and keep your Heaven open. You've got to be forgiving and loving, repent when you miss it, "He that begun a work in you, shall continue it until the day of Jesus Christ." (Philippians 1:6) God knows you are a work in progress but that doesn't mean you can't forgive, stick to the Word and apply it. In order to go to Heaven you have to repent, no sinner will enter Heaven that's why the life of repentance is key. You can live a secret life all you want, but without repentance your life will still have stain on it.

What is repentance? Acknowledging before God that you have missed it, and you are sorry, at the same time you are telling satan you are not his, see a person who refuse to repent is full of pride, God resist the proud and he exalt the humble, humble yourself before God and he will exalt you (James 4:6-10). When you live a life of repentance it shows that you depend on God to be a better believer.

The only person who refuses to repent before God is satan he even exalted himself before God (Isaiah 14:12-18) he said he is better than God while God is the one who created him.

As a born again believer, you bear on your body the marks of the Lord Jesus Christ (Galatians 6:17), live the life of repentance and mean it, you will see how your life will change. Let go of those people and grudges you are holding in your heart, repent of all the wrong you have done in public or in secret before God, "Everything is naked before His sight." (Hebrews 4:13) He knows what you have done He just wants you to acknowledge it so satan doesn't have room to accuse you before God. When God is set to bless you, the Bible calls Him the accuser of the brothers who accuses you day and night (Revelation 12:10). Can you imagine that satan has nothing better to do than to monitor your life, trying to find something to accuse you with before God so God can be restrained by that accusation not to bless you? Satan looks for opportunities like that to challenge God, by trying to make Him look like He is violating His own Word, that's why repentance is a warfare sometimes, but it is worth more fighting than hurting. So decide today to live a life of repentance and watch what God will do in your life.

CHAPTER THIRTEEN
THE POWER OF WORDS

⇄

"It is the spirit that quicken; the flesh profit nothing: the words that I speak to you, they spirit, and they are life" (John 6:63).

It's amazing how words can be a force, something simple yet powerful (James 3:8). Words have an important meaning in our lives, Jesus Christ told His disciples the words that you speak are life and they are spirit, in other words, your words can bring life in any areas that seem dead. Also they are spirit—that means nothing can take place in the natural unless it was first manifested in the spirit. John the Baptist father's mouth was shut because God did not want him to spoil the coming of John the Baptist, he was full of unbelief and God wouldn't allow his negative confession to mess up what he was about to do, and he was dumb (Luke 1:20-22) until the day he was asked to name the child (Luke 1:57-68), can you imagine that. God himself is showing us here the importance of words, "Do not let corrupt communication proceed out of your mouth." (Ephesians 4:29) You are not born again of the corruptible seed but of the incorruptible seed, which is Jesus Christ, and by the Word of God, which lives and abides forever (1 Peter 1:23).

Do not take your words lightly, many things that happen to us either good or bad, are because of the contribution of our words. "Oh Lord you are killing me," "I'm dying to go," "My feet are killing me," They sound like nothing, but be careful, because once you speak, it will start manifesting. Choose your words carefully —they can cost you. "I'm poor…" don't say that, God said "Let the poor say I'm rich," if you feel sick, "By his stripes I'm healed," (Isaiah 53:5), start confessing God's Words over your life now. Do not wait until you get into a situation because it is hard to build during the flood, in other words, it's hard to build your faith all of a sudden, it's a process to get your faith to a certain level and consistency is key.

Jesus Christ said He had to work while it was day (John 9:4); that means darkness will come at some point in your life. He knew he would be crucified someday, He knew He would have to carry the cross and be hanged. If Jesus Christ waited to ask people to repent, or if He waited to tell them He was the Son of God, it would have been hard for them to witness the aftermath. He started to tell them all that ahead of time, so when He was on the cross, no one would doubt Him, but because He did it while it was day and when darkness came the words were working to His advantage and they remembered what He told them long ago.

Watch who you associate with, if you don't change your environment sooner or later you become like your environment through the power of association. Jesus Christ said somebody was going to betray Him and His disciples went in chock mode, but the Bible said as Judas Iscariot ate the bread satan entered in the bread (John 13:27). When you keep listening to the wrong things sooner or later that thought will enter you and start to dominate your life.

Do not spend time around things that can influence your life in a bad way. Now bad can be defined in many ways, smoking weed is bad for me, because my body is the temple of the Holy Spirit (1 Corinthians 6:19), but to somebody else it is a good thing to do that, it is bad for me to fornicate because sex before marriage is a sin, but to somebody it's good, also the Bible states out of the flesh dwell no good things because the flesh is never satisfied, but if you can't contain, let them marry: for it is better to marry than to burn (1 Corinthians 7:9) you get my point. Look at it in God's point of view and not your own point of view.

The birth of Jesus Christ is the result of words spoken by the prophets through the leading of the Holy Spirit, today we are witnessing the speech "words" of Dr. King come alive, blacks and whites working, eating, building families together that is the power of the spoken words. Never underestimate your words—they carry results, speak life today and not death.

CHAPTER FOURTEEN
CHANGE YOUR THINKING, BELIEVE IN THE LORD

⇄

God made Moses a god over Pharaoh and Aaron his prophet (Exodus 7:1), God has made you a god over satan and any deity over your family. You were not created by God for satan to tell you what to do, but you were created by God to tell satan what to do. See you have been given permission to use the name of Jesus Christ. The Bible says, "At the name of Jesus Christ every knees shall bow... and every tongue shall confess that Jesus Christ is Lord." (Philippians 2:9-11) Is satan a name? Is chaos a name? Is divorce a name? You get the point—they shall bow to you.

You are in covenant with the God who formed this world under chaos, and not when everything was perfect, even in chaos the hand of God is seen. You were created from such authority because you have the DNA of God through Jesus Christ. Chaos shall never amaze you, but it should inspire you, because in chaos is where you see the hand of God in another dimension. God created the world in chaos, He made us out of the dirt (Genesis 2:7) and yet the Bible declares we are made in His image (Genesis 1:26-27). Chaos is not a thing to fear, because God will surely show up and show you that He is God indeed.

The crossing of the Red Sea was a chaotic sight, it looked like a matter of life and death; it looked like a death sentence if Pharaoh caught them, but God spoke. When God gives an order that means He has a plan. Moses thought it was the end, but God is not limited, He told Moses stretch out your rod (Exodus 14:21-31), who could have known a rod can part the sea, but God gave the command and it was so. All you need in the time of chaos is the Word from God and that settles it, Moses thought it was over, so did the rest of the leaders, but not in the sight of God. His Word will never fall to the ground (1 Samuel 3:19). You will have to change your thinking and trust Him all the way, and you will be surprised in the God you believe in. There is no limit with God, no limit at all.

CHAPTER FIFTEEN
WHERE IS YOUR HEART?

⇄

Every man is equipped to lead his family in the right direction, every blessing comes with a responsibility, and anywhere God places you as a steward—requires work (Luke 12:48). God blessed Abraham because He knew he will teach his children after God (Genesis 18:17-19). As a father, you have the duty to lead your children in the right way and train up your children in the way they should go, so when they grow they shall not depart from what they have been taught (Proverbs 22:6).

Show your children every testimony that God manifests and has manifested in your life, as proof that the God you serve is a mighty God. Engage your children in your spiritual walk as a training ground to maintain their spiritual walk and relationship with God. The only reason Isaac could stay on course, was because his father Abraham taught him. He taught him how to pray, how to fast, and how to believe God at His Word (Genesis 24:62-63). If we can get back to the beginning, our children's future will be in great shape.

The reason this generation is failing is because we (the last generation) have failed them. I hear people say, "Grandma and Grandpa did this or that," but what have you done for the generation after you? We owe it to our children and our grandchildren. When God blessed Abraham He did it knowing that Abraham would leave something for his son Isaac and his grandchildren (Proverbs 13:22). The reason we are witnessing what we are witnessing now, is because of either ignorance or selfishness. Families are supposed to leave a legacy so strong that once they have tapped into this lifestyle: the families shouldn't witness divorce. Because of lust and lack of knowledge they have taken an escape route and have decided to divorce instead of working it out and in turn it has ruined many destinies.

As believers we ought to get upset with perfect hatred when the attack is over families because we ought to know better. Our children are a blessing and not a curse (Isaiah 8:18), the Bible says "They shall fight with the enemy at the gate," (Psalm 127:5). If you don't teach them, the devil will use them to turn against you. That will not be your portion, in the name of Jesus Christ. Where your heart is, there is your treasure (Matthew 6:21). Are your children, your wife and yourself a treasure to each other? Are you treasuring your family, are you taking time to pray and fast for your family, are you teaching your children wrong from right? Your children shouldn't be influenced by their friends or outsiders (Psalms 1:1), are you teaching your children to trust God with everything (Psalms 1:2-3)?

We have an epidemic going on, under aged children getting pregnant and we are mad at them, we shouldn't be when we have not taught them about all those things. The Word of God must be brought back in our families, Joshua said "As for me and my house; we shall serve The Lord," (Joshua 24:15). We go to church but church is not in us, we pick subjects to learn from, we shouldn't shy from topics that are core to the things we are dealing with, the Word of God is for our spiritual growth, and correction. We don't like to touch what corrects us; many people like what endorse them to keep acting like a fool. Without knowing it, it's at the cost of your destiny and your life.

We have been lied to, we can have harmony in our households. Isaiah 32:18 says that God has given us peaceable habitations. You and your children shall dwell in unity. There is no place in the Bible where Jesus Christ had a misunderstanding with His Father, He said He does the will of the Father. It is our duty to know the will of God for our children and lead them in the right direction. A house divided against itself cannot stand (Matthew 12:25). See, we have allowed ignorance to bring chaos in our houses and confusion in relationship with our children, God is not the author of confusion, "But of power, love, and a sound mind," (2 Timothy 1:7). Yes we have made mistakes, but through the Word of God— any bad mistakes can be reversed. He restores the years that were wasted by satan or our ignorance (Joel 2:25). Ignorance is not an excuse that's why the truth needs to be told. We can live Heaven on earth. This is the plan God has for you and me; we don't need to get to Heaven to enjoy life. You can enjoy Heaven here on earth. That's what God wants for you and me.

It never pleases God when a family goes into chaos. It doesn't glorify Him. What kind of God would He be if He takes pleasure in your sorrow? His best interest at heart, is to perfect what concerns you (Psalms 138:8). Why is that? Because God wants you to enjoy life as He desires for your children and grandchildren.

CHAPTER SIXTEEN
DON'T HOLD BACK YOUR BLESSING

⇄

You will be surprised how many parents hate to see their children be better than them. They want them to make it, but not surpass them in achievement. Some parents act like brothers or sisters in jealousy over their children's success. Your children have to be better than you, there is no competition, you have to be joyful when your children do better than you did. At the end of the day the joy is yours because they carry your name. The fact that you have spoken or carry that feeling in your heart could be the reason why your children are struggling in certain areas.

Some parents can see their children struggling to get married, going to jail time after time, or dying one after another; yet they do nothing about it. Keeping quiet, they run to the pastor for comfort. Yes, it hurts to go through that, but there comes a time you've got to take matters into your own hand, spiritually, in prayer and fasting. There are prayers only you can pray for them because you know how you are feeling in that moment. You ought to be mad spiritually when your children are struggling—they should not suffer what you suffered. There are things God will not reveal to your pastor but to you alone; because God wants to protect your privacy.

There are prayers that God doesn't answer unless you take your own initiative. I'm sure Hannah went to see the man of God before for prayer for the fruit of the womb, but nothing happened until she cried out to God on her own and God answered her with a prophetic pregnancy. Samuel was born as a result of her earnest prayer, the same Prophet Samuel who was one of the greatest in Israel (1 Samuel 1:9-23). Take charge of your life by trusting God. Jabez's mother named him *sorrow*, in other words, all his life was going to witness sorrow, can you imagine that all your life is the embodiment of sorrow; that must hurt. Instead of dwelling on that, he took the issue into his own hands and cried out to God and God blessed him and answered his request. He took it into his hands and blamed no one (1 Chronicles 4:9-10).

The blaming game gets nowhere, it makes matters complicated. Be your number one investor—invest in you with knowledge and revelation in the Word of God, by listening to tapes and reading books and doing your own Bible study. You will be surprised on the things we invest in many times. We invest sometimes in the things that do not build us up and neglect what builds us up. Your thinking needs to change, as you embark in unleashing the defense against any force that will try to attack your children as they have done to you. Behold and don't hold back your blessing through fear, instead celebrate you and your children by giving glory to God.

CHAPTER SEVENTEEN
LIFE

⇄

Life is full of surprises. When you were born again, God did not promise you there will not be any issues; but He did promise you that He will not leave you nor forsake you. God will not cast off His people, neither will He forsake His inheritance (Psalms 94:14) because He knows problem will come and go. In the course of life, and any problem you may encounter, God has the solution for it already. One of the reason God allows you to encounter challenges, is to remind us that He is the only one who can help us—your friends have limit, whosoever you may trust in the flesh and blood has limit, but God is the only one who has no limit.

The worse mistake anybody can make in life is to doubt God at His Word, because "The Word of God is quick and powerful and sharper than any two edge sword," (Hebrews 4:12). What a sword does is penetrate places when nothing else can penetrate, but God said His Word can penetrate any area in your life that needs healing, restoration, or deliverance; that's why it's dangerous not to take God at His Word.

Anything you face in life can be fixed with the Word of God, "In the beginning was the Word and the Word was with God," Even God Himself, before He does something, starts with the Word (John 1:1-3). "The earth was without form and void... and God said, let there be light and there was light," see, God is showing us that words have power (Genesis 1:3-9), life and death is in power of words of the tongue (Proverbs 18:21). Be careful what you speak it may cost you. Success is for those who take on challenges and failure is for those who run from challenges. Your success comes by believing God and your failure comes by doubting His Word.

The worse mistake anybody can make in life is to doubt God at His Word, because the Word of God is sharper than any two edged sword and it is the fixer of any answer you need in life.

CHAPTER EIGHTEEN
SPIRITUAL FOOD

⇄

Food is important in anybody's diet; we all love eating food, and when we engage in it, we definitely feel good by doing so. There is a reason why food plays a very important role in our bodies and for our human system. God does not create something without a purpose, everything God created has a purpose—to benefit us. Now if you choose to use what was meant as good for you, and use it for bad, then the consequence is your doing, it's not God's fault but your own.

Spiritual food is no different than natural food; if you eat the wrong food, it may kill you spiritually where nothing matter to you anymore. Many people have been fed the wrong spiritual food, (i.e. been taught the wrong doctrine of the Word of God through tradition and lack of revelation,) and it has silenced their faith and hope in God in certain areas of their life. "The tradition of men have made the Word of God of none effect," (Mark 7:13-14). This tells you that the Word of God has effect, but a wrong doctrine can make it of no effect in your life because of unbelief. False doctrine causes you to doubt and reject the truth that must set you free (Colossians 2:8-10).

You need the food that gives you the power of right believing. Many people are suffering today because they have been digesting the wrong spiritual food—the wrong teaching of the Word of God. The Word of God is there to set you free, not to keep you bound. God's Word liberates and does not keep you oppressed. If you are witnessing this, it's because of wrong teaching or wrong believing, when you are not taught well, you are bound to fail, failure is not an issue of tries, it's an issue of lacking knowledge and revelation —not information, information has limit but revelation supersedes information.

Revelation gives you what information can't give you, that is why revelation is key in a believer's life, John was able to give us the glimpse of the end times because of revelation, the Bible would have been incomplete without the book of Revelation. But John the Baptist questioned Jesus Christ ministry because of the information he had "are you the one or shall we look for another," (Luke 7:19-22). But by revelation he could say I must decrease and let Him increase, He is the One—I'm just here to prepare his way. Change your diet today. Choose to be in the right church and do your own Bible study for your own growth, if you want to be in good health: eat the right food, if you want to overcome many obstacles in life: invest in eating the right spiritual food—right teaching that edifying your inner man (Ephesians 4:11-12).

Some people go to church but do not believe in healing, prosperity, walking in love, long life, and so forth. They believe in everything else except that which is good. They believe in sickness, they believe in poverty, they believe eye for an eye, they believe in untimely death… Yet God has promised you long life (Psalm 91:16), the reason they don't believe that, is the result of wrong spiritual food you are being fed, you become what you eat.

Change your diet and you will be well. If you want to believe God for a great life, listen to messages and testimonies that boost your spiritual strength, never get comfortable with the things of God, because God is not the God of formula but He is the God of result. Make a decision and choose to change your diet, don't mind your critics, but mind where you are going and silence them when you reach your destination. You don't have to blend in, in order to mount on wings of eagles, you don't have to be popular, an eagle soars high and alone, but it achieves great things even though being alone. God said you shall mount with wings of eagle (Isaiah 40:31) so why are you in the chicken coop? Decide what you want to eat; you choose between dead meat and fresh food, you make the choice. Remember you are responsible for your spiritual diet.

CHAPTER NINETEEN
PROSPERITY

⇄

"Honor the Lord with your substance, and with the first fruits [Tithe] of all your increase:

"So shall your barns [bank account, house] be filled with plenty, and your presses [career and business will never run out of ideas] shall burst out with new wine." (Proverbs 3:9-10)

The message of prosperity has been a message of many controversies among the unbelievers and the doubters, both in the church and outside of the church. Prosperity, in the church, shouldn't be a debate—it should be the way of life. The world does not argue their prosperity, you don't hear billionaires say, "Prosperity is bad," Only those who are low minded thinkers who think it's bad.

If prosperity is bad, why is it that America and other countries are trying to have a surplus in their economy, they should stop thinking about it, if prosperity was that bad. God wants the church to prosper, and prosperity is from God. The world will never support the church because they are under a demonic system. Their goal is to delay the move of the gospel, the world will never relate to the church because we don't share the same vision and values, the things of God are foolish to the world because they are spiritually discerned (1 Corinthians 2:14). That's why God released the ideas that make the gospel to be within reach by using venues such as Facebook, Google, Skype, TV's, and so forth, even though it makes it possible for the gospel to be within reach, still the church of Jesus Christ has a long way to go, because the believers are the only one who can further the gospel—not the world. In the world they rather spend $1 million on a party than pay their tithe, but in the Kingdom you tithe out of that $1 million and still get blessed because it is done in obedience.

I was in prayer and I asked God why the message of prosperity so controversial in the church, the answer He gave me was so simple but powerful, He said the reason people fight the message of prosperity is because they don't have the glimpse of heaven. Wow, it dawned on me: God said you shall witness heaven on earth, there is no mortgage in Heaven, there is no pay as you go in Heaven, pavement of gold, no sickness and everything is whole and beautiful, I see why the Bible says, "Beloved, I desire in all things you be in good health even as your soul prospers," (3 John 1:2). That's all Heaven has. God want you to prosper. He wants you to enjoy life.

Stop trying to explain to the world why you do what you do, the world does not understand you because they do not know the God you serve (1 John 3:1); Without prosperity in the church it makes the sacrifice of Jesus Christ on the cross half complete, the resurrection restored all. He is the groom of the church, the groom is supposed to take care of the bride and not the bride taking care of the groom only. When you have the vision God has given you, the groom will provide for the bride. Let's stop diluting the Word of God with our feelings, and lack of understanding. God is not led by feelings, but by faith: for it is impossible to please God without faith (Hebrews 11:6). So prosperity is the will of God, Jesus Christ became poor so you become rich (2 Corinthians 8:9), so stop fighting the prosperity message, just receive it and believe it, also do your own Bible study and let the Holy Spirit open your eyes, that you see what God wants you to see.

When your bills are due why don't you just go to those you owe and pray in tongues or just pray and tell them I believe I receive? Because they don't understand that and you don't want to hear their cold response either. All they want is cash money, if you don't have money how are you going to take care of it? Think about when you are prospering, no bill collector will be disturbing you, no car financing company will be calling you that they want to repo your car. Proverbs 22:7 says, "The rich rule over the poor, and the borrower is slave to the lender."

Many people work for the rich and not for themselves. That's why God wants you to be rich. I don't know about you, I don't like to struggle, Jesus Christ did everything for us, why not take advantage of His promises and enjoy it. I'm not going to work and give my money to those who don't finance the gospel. I want to believe the Word of God so that money will be working for me when God is blessing me and not me working for money.

I want my children to go to elite, godly schools of their choice, I want to eat what I want and go on vacation debt free. Doesn't it make you feel good when you are living that lifestyle? It gives you time to spend with God because you are worry free, you shall be the lender and not the borrower (Deuteronomy 15:6) these are the promises of God: above only and not beneath (Deuteronomy 28:13), blessed going out and bless coming in (Deuteronomy 28:6). These promises apply only to those who pay their tithes and offerings, because God is the God of order. Let's do everything "decently and in order," (1 Corinthians 14:40). There is no short cut with God, if you are not a tither and don't give offerings you are missing out on certain blessings. The gospel, at best, deals with the whole man, not only his soul but also his body, not only his spiritual well-being, but his material being as well.

Some people and churches will never witness the pinnacle of wealth unless you give yourself wholly to God and make Him your sole provider, your helper and your all. The more you look to people for a hand out you have just insulted God, remember He said He is a jealous God (Exodus 31:14, Exodus 20:5, Deuteronomy 4:24, Deuteronomy 5:9, Joshua 24:19). God should be your only Hope and your only resource. He said His Word shall not return void (Isaiah 55:11). Place your hope in God and look to Him only and you will not be disappointed.

CHAPTER TWENTY
EXAMINE THE GROUND
YOU SOW YOUR SEED INTO

⇄

"Beloved, believe not every spirit, but try the spirits whether they are of God: because many false prophets are gone out into the world." (1 John 4:1)

Your seed is a part of you. It is your sweat and the reward of your labor. Be careful where you sow your seed, not every ministry that you see on TV is for Jesus Christ; some ministries are not for God anymore. It could have been a good ministry before, it may not be now. In some ministries the presence of God is not there anymore, because the leaders have refused to repent of their evil ways and the sheep are suffering because of their disobedience, whatever you sow on a ground like that; it will not bring fruit, because it is a stony ground. When you realize you have sown your seed on bogus ground, pray Proverbs 6:31 aggressively with fire and authority, in order to be restored what is owed to you.

Some ministries profess Jesus Christ but are part of a coven, whatever you sow on that ground, it will bring you only backward, instead of going forward; because many ministries are connected to satan and witches and wizard in quest of obtaining counterfeit power. In these ministries, their job is to delay people's destinies and callings. But the time is coming where God will expose them one by one. Many so called "churches" are going to close. Why? Because they will be exposed by the light, God has been merciful to those churches to change their ways, but the time is coming where the wrath of God will be seen in those so called churches. It's very important to pray about a church before you go there or before you give your money there, lack of doing that can cost you your life and finances. I tell you this because it was revealed to me by the Spirit of God. Even a farmer before he plants a seed, has to make sure the ground is fit to produce the crop he wants, it is a principal both natural and spiritual.

I had to go through a one year of deliverance from a ministry I was helping out. The so called "servant of god" came from another state and said the Lord sent me to Chicago because of the cry of the saints in the city, I was naïve and thirsty to do God's work. I was there for a year helping out; I have never preached there, I was just a helper; later on I did some Spiritual search, because a lot of things were not adding up based on the scriptures of the Word of God and the Spirit of God revealed to me that servant was not sent by God, the servant was working with marine powers; the servant did miracles like God was with that servant, the magicians did the same with Moses (Exodus 8:3-7), but time came when Moses serpent swallowed all of their serpent (Exodus 7:8-12)-(Exodus 8:16-19) the magicians meet their limit.

That ministry made me broke because the papers I had signed gave them the legal right in the spirit to collect all my money and favor. In the realm of the spirit it was considered a form of a covenant, so my money was going to them in the Spirit, my check would disappear before I could view my account, money will disappear out of my pocket and accounts, I had to fast and pray because I was losing too much money. That's when my eyes were opened, I had a dream and in that dream I had a bag full of gold coins and I saw a hand going in taking those gold coins, but regardless how much they took the bag was not getting empty then I woke up. I saw the hand taking money out of it, but I couldn't see the face of the person who was taking the money. But the hand looked familiar and the Holy Spirit gave me some prayers and instruction to break that evil covenant, it wasn't easy; because it was a full year of giving, but glory be to God, the covenant was broken and everything was restored.

Please don't be moved by emotion, instead be moved by the leading of the Holy Spirit, regardless of the need, make sure you hear from God. Many shepherds don't have any program in their church to teach their sheep how to hear from God, that's why satan is having a field day with the sheep that do not know the voice of the good shepherd, this needs to be taught.

You are the light of the world, let your light shine. Shine in darkness. Don't let darkness rule you, you rule the darkness. God ruled the darkness, He said let there be light and there was light. Let God give you light in your giving and where you fellowship.

CHAPTER TWENTY-ONE
THE TITHE FACTOR

⇄

God says in Malachi 3:10 pay your tithes and offering, "That there may there be meat in my house…" and He "…will open windows of Heaven and pour you out a blessing and there is not room enough to receive it." When you read that did you see the name of your pastor there? I don't think so, because your pastor did not come with it, it's not his idea, it is God's idea and He is the author of the tithe. As you read it saying bring the tithes and offering to the house "Church" not eat it. *Meat* there refers to provision, your tithe and offering provide for the house of God, when you don't obey God on this promise you are called a robber, I don't want Heaven to record me as a robber of God's provision, I pray not.

If you give or don't give God will always take care of his house—the only person missing out is you and not God. Choose you today life or death and let heaven record your decision (Deuteronomy 30:19). When you rob God, you are inviting death upon your life because you have just lifted the protection off your life. You pay your tithe on all illegal wages and offered based on your own will and that act of obedience will rebuke satan's attack against you and it will stop what satan tries to destroy in your life

I don't see why people fight to give their tithes and offering, God knows why He put it in place. When you obey, you are placing a demand in the spirit to cover the natural. We don't argue with the IRS over our taxes, we pay it and it is used to build schools, fix roads and so forth, well your tithes is your tax in the spirit, it covers what the natural can't give you without Heaven's consent. I thank God for grace because it's by grace you can do all these, pray to God to give you grace to be consistent with your tithe and offering—it will bless you. "I have never seen the righteous forsaken or his seed begging for bread," (Psalms 37:25). Your tithes and offerings makes you in right standing with God to partake of those privileges only a tither gets to do, when you align with the scripture.

Are you ready to make a shift now after reading this? God is for you, but the question is, are you ready for God? Malachi is the only place where God wants you to prove Him of what you are capable of, nowhere in the Bible He says to prove Him except in Malachi—that should ring a bell. The tither can't beg, no way, God promised you He will open windows of Heaven and pour you a blessing; there is no other option but to be blessed.

Now don't tithe to get rich, the tithe it's not meant for that, do you pay taxes to be rich? Not so, you pay it because it contributes to areas that work for your advantage, so is the tithe. From now on, make up your mind to be on God's side and pay your tithes and offering. You will not regret it, it's not easy to live that lifestyle of obedience, but by believing God's Word it is doable. The only reason people don't tithe is because they don't believe God's Word nor trust God to bless them in return, if they did, tithing and giving offerings wouldn't be a problem.

Abraham was blessed because he was a faithful tither and giver, and God blessed him with plenty riches in return just by following the Word of God, you can do the same and be blessed like faithful Abraham (Galatians 3:1-14). It delights God when you are blessed, He takes pleasure in your prosperity (Psalms 35:27), that is God's desire for you.

God may give you a certain grace; you come to the point of repentance, the goodness of God leads to repentance. Now when you don't tithe or give offerings, God can't trust you with big money unless you prove you are trustworthy. What makes you think when you have more money you will tithe when you can't tithe when you have little (Luke 16:10).

The woman who gave her last mite—she had little, yet gave her all (Mark 12:42). It could be she paid her bills and all she had left was her tithe, could it be after she paid her mortgage or rent all she had left was either to pay her car note or her tithe and she decided to pay her tithe instead, that gesture of obedience moved Jesus Christ, because it was not a random act, it was an act of faith and obedience, obedience is better than sacrifice (1 Samuel 15:22) God knew her heart as well, also He knows yours. I doubt that woman's finances remained the same, she proved before God to be trustworthy and faithful. If the widow woman obeyed Elijah and fed him first and she never ran out of oil and never went hungry the rest of her life (1 Kings 17:10-16), how much when you obey God the outcome will always be greater.

What is interested about the situation of the woman who gave her is mite is that many people gave, but to those who gave Jesus Christ made it clear that they all gave but He said the woman gave her all and the others gave their abundance isn't abundance better than a mite, to God it's not the abundance that counts but the act of obedience, fear of God and reverence. Could it be they were giving but not tithing, could they have given as a tradition and not as an act of faith, the Bible says, "whatsoever that is not of faith is sin," (Romans 14:23). Jesus Christ said they gave out of their abundance, why make the mite sound bigger than the rest of them? God is not moved by your giving, he is moved by your obedience and your faith in Him. Why drive a fancy car, and live in a big home and you can't pay your tithe? See, you don't have to impress anybody, all you need to impress is God. When you impress God He will shock you and bless you beyond your wildest imagination.

I don't know if that woman had anything left to eat, I don't know if she had transportation back home, but she trusted God and God rewarded her big time, you can't obey God and not see the hand of God in your life. God is so good He can't disappoint those who regard to Him.

Look at Achan he brought death upon his family because he stole what belonged to God (Joshua 7:10-25), the tithe is sacred and it belongs to God, back then they used to stone people, thank God we are not in those days, now in our days we have a spiritual death, when you don't tithe you are killing things around you spiritually, the car brakes down, the dish washer goes out and so forth. Verse 21 Achan saw a nice outfit and he took it, maybe you saw a nice watch, and used your tithe for that, how many people until now use the tithe to buy those things and he said they are hid in the earth in the midst of my tent "House" many people have their tithes hidden in the stock market, bonds, savings accounts and checking accounts. If that is your tithe you are using to invest or to make your bank account fatter and make yourself look flashy, I advise you to give it back to the house of God, because you will lose it and it may cost you your life because the protection is lifted up as a covering in the spiritual realm, whether you know it or not. Let me tell you a little about me:

One day I used my tithe, I thought I will be fine. I said in my heart I will pay it next time. Guess what happened? My car broke down with a repair that cost the same as the amount of the tithe. I thought I will learned my lesson. A few years later I used my tithe again for a shirt that was on sale and I really wanted it. Guess what? My car was broken into and everything was stolen in it and the insurance refused to cover it even though I had full coverage, guess what the repair cost me... the same amount as the tithe, this isn't coincidence it is God speaking. Ever since then, I have become a faithful tither regardless the issue, I tithe and God can trust me with money now and doors have been opening for me left and right because I have obeyed the command of God. He has no choice but to bless me. There are people I know who have encountered worse because the protection was lifted up.

Don't plan a picnic without checking the weather, you don't know when you step out there what satan has planned against you. This isn't to make satan seem powerful, not at all. It is a spiritual covenant and it requires your participation and obedience in order to be active. Because to deal with satan you need a greater power and that power belongs to God. The tithe is there to put the hand of God in motion for you whenever satan tries to do something against you. God by His grace will protect you to a certain extent but He can't help you when you have lifted away the protection. He can't rebuke satan when you have not engaged God to rebuke satan through your tithe and obedience. Your tithe could save your marriage against evil attatcks, your children getting wrongly accused, untimely death, and so forth; it says your vine will not bring forth fruit before it's time (that is premature death) and you will not reap loss in your investment, only profit. All of these are covenant promises found in Malachi 3:6-12 for us to apply in our lives—a resource given to us by God for our use, no wonder some envy the world while the world is supposed to envy you, because of lack of knowing what the tithe can do, you have settled for less. As a man thinks so is he (Proverbs 23:7).

So if certain things are not working for you, you've got to wonder are you tithing and giving offerings? Seek the face of God, stop accusing the devil and giving him credit like he is a big shot, you are your own problem sometimes and not the devil. The devil is not more powerful than you; you are more than a conquerer in Jesus Christ (Romans 8:37) so why are you letting the devil mess with you if the devil is the case. And for those who says that God is good, that is good, but since you have become famous and successful, making beaucoup money I want to tell you stop boasting about God when you are not giving your tithes into the church, it is obedience that counts not your mere words to act holy and spiritual. Everyone was created by God to have a home church so you can be a vessel God can use for His glory for the advancement of the kingdom. God made you wealthy; what have you done for God, your charitable donation, is not your tithe, your tithe is the 10th of your gross and not net and it belongs to the local church, and not your bank accounts, trust funds and so forth but to the church you are planted. Don't think the pastor will take your money, don't worry about that, just do your part and he will have to deal with God on that. Start living in obedience and stop listening to your accounts or edge funds manager in order to walk in disobedience because they want their share.

God had blessed King David so much and that he was thinking about building God a house, but David never acted on his thought. It was a nice thought, but a thought without action is just a thought and not impact. So God visited Nathan the Prophet and told him about King David, how he has become so comfortable in his palace and forgot everything God has done for him, he has a great name now, and gave him victory over his enemies and so forth (2 Samuel 7:1-29). Have you become so comfortable that you forgot to build

God's house, but in the mean time you are building mansions for yourself with the money that was meant to build God's House? Did you forget from where God has delivered you from? Did you forget sleeping in the car and never getting sick, did you forget about having no closet of your own, did you forget that He gave you hope for the future when you thought there was no future, did you forget when you had no car to get to work? But He has blessed you now with plenty, did you forget when no one believed in you but God, did you forget that He was the one who gave you that first job and contract, did you forget that He was the one who gave you that peace when you had nothing to show for, did you forget when you had no friends and God was your only Friend?

But now your friends are more important than supporting God's house, are you spending more time with them than with Him, they take most of your time and He is your last resort only in trouble, but never in good times. And God is saying refocus just like He told King David, remember those times and look up. My house is in need of your obedience of the tithe, it is Mine and not yours, whenever you dishonor what is Mine, you dishonor Me. You honor the government of the world by paying your taxes on time; you fear them more than you fear Me. You take care of everybody else except Me, when my turn comes I AM discounted, don't you know that I AM connected to the tithe, the Tithe and Me are one, because it is a command connected to My Word. Refocus, let me be first and bring to my house what belongs to Me, the tithe. The tithe is Mine. Since you have a name now you have surely forgotten about

Me. If you love me, obey My Word and bring the tithe in My house.

CHAPTER TWENTY-TWO
NEVER ALONE

⇄

"Behold, the hour comes, yeah, is now come, that you shall be scattered, every man to his own, and shall leave me alone: and yet I am not alone, because the Father is with me." (John 16:32).

Being alone is a good thing sometimes, it's not a bad thing at all, Paul said, "Follow me as I followed Jesus Christ," (1 Corinthians 11:1). I love that statement he gave, it's very empowering. There is nobody greater to follow than Jesus Christ, Jesus Christ often took time off from everything and went on a quiet moment spending time with God, and when He was done He was refreshed and renewed better than ever.

There was an occasion in the book of John when Jesus Christ said that He is never alone, the Father is with Him (John 16:32). The truth of the matter is you are never alone, the Holy Spirit is with you. Doesn't Jesus Christ say, "I will not leave you comfortless I will send you a comforter who will be with you," (John 14:18) and

(John 14:26), that's all you need to know that you are comforted on every side by the Holy Spirit that you are never alone (John 14:18), Jesus Christ said I'm always with you until the end of the world (Matthew 28:20). Is the world over? No, then Jesus Christ is with you, also He said, "I will never leave you nor forsake you," (Hebrews 13:5). These are powerful promises, that you are never alone. King David said, "When I make my bed in hell you are with me," (Psalms 139:8). All King David was saying was, even in my terrible moment that feels like hell you are with me, because God does not fellowship with hell.

God is for you who then can be against you? Lack of knowing who is with you has caused many people to be in fear, "Fear not I'm with you," Jesus Christ has overcome the world, greater is He that is in you than he who is in the world, you are not alone; don't you fear a thing. One of the greatest achievements in life is to know who is with you. King David was able to overcome Goliath with a sling-shot and a stone because he knew who was with him (1 Samuel 17:45-46), it was a fearful moment for others to embark in a fight like that, but to King David it was as nothing because he knew who was with him, he was not alone, the others feared because they felt alone and helpless, I got news for you, "Look up from whence comes your help, your help comes from The Lord... He that keep you do not slumber nor sleep," (Psalms 121:1-8).

Don't be afraid of loosing your life when you sleep, you serve a God that does not sleep, He is awake 24/7 and 365 days a year, if God slept, everything would collapse—that is true and fact, He is fully awake for you any time you need Him, you are not alone;

God is with you, I want you to know that. Take fear out of the equation and replace it with the presence of God and your life will never be the same. When you fear, you limit yourself from the help you need. God is your help—why fear. Job invited chaos in his home because of fear, "The things I fear the most has come upon me," (Job 3:25). He could have used that same effort he used to fear for divine protection over his children. Fear is not pleasing to God, because when you fear you are telling God that He's not able to handle such issues, while He actually is the only help you have. Remember this: you are never alone, God is with you always.

CHAPTER TWENTY-THREE
STUDY TO SHOW YOURSELF APPROVED

$$\rightleftarrows$$

"Study to show yourself approved into God, a workman that needs not to be ashamed, rightly dividing the word of truth" (2 Timothy 2:15).

It is the desire of God that you study His Word, the Word of God is not just for pastors, deacons, prophets and evangelists only; but it is for everyone. People increase in knowledge in everything else except in the Word of God. Take new course to increase your flexibility to get a better job, don't just read a certain book because you love the author and so forth. None of those books, classes or experience will unlock many mysteries in your life like the Bible will. The Bible is our way of life. When you go to the hospital and someone is diagnosed with a certain malady, what does the doctor do? He opens a medical book and in that book it tells him what kind of medication and what dose the person needs to be given and what period of time in order to see the result of the treatment. The Bible does the same thing.

Whatever medicine you need it's in the Bible, the Word of God. The study of the Word is your guidelines in life. Many revelations from the Word of God have not yet been revealed because of the saint's immaturity over the things of God. But the time is coming when the Word of God will be the only choice in life, without it all the problems you face will never be unlocked unless you apply the Word of God, because the Word is life.

When I come across people and we are having a conversation, I often hear them ask me if I'm a pastor; I ask them why, then they give me their reasons. I had observed that for some time and later came to understand that many people believe that Bible revelation or study of the Bible is reserved for Pastors only. No! The Bible is available to whomsoever, that is one of the lies people have allowed themselves to believe.

I had to grow spiritually because I got tired of waiting for someone to pray for me, when I called the church I couldn't get in touch with the pastor or his assistant, there is a waiting list to see the man of God on weekdays but could see him after service for prayer on Wednesdays or Sundays, for some reason I was in need of prayer on weekdays when they were not reachable, I came to understand that. The pastor has other things to do as well and I have to respect that. Instead of being offended, I changed my mind set. There are prayers your pastor can pray for you and the situation will change, but many of the prayers you should be able to handle by yourself. Bible knowledge is a must for everybody, that's why it is important to buy CD's and books and grow in the wisdom and Word of God. The CD's and books help you to understand certain revelation, but the growth of you as a person and with your relationship with God comes when you study the Bible, fast, and pray - seeking his face that's when you grow. So don't just buy the CD's and read books but do the other things as well. If you can dedicate two days per week in prayer, fasting and study the Word of God, your spiritual life will be at another dimension.

If you have an emergency and your pastor is out of town, you will not wait for him to come take care of the situation while you could have done so on your own. You and your pastor both have the same authority, the only difference between you and your pastor is he is bold in his prayer, not wishing something will happen but believing it will happen. Remember you have the same spirit that was operating on Jesus Christ, and in order to get to that level you need to study the Word of God and spend time in prayer. Your growth is for the benefit of the church and for your calling. There are revelations that God has not released yet on many ministries or the saints because of their spiritual immaturity, you got to grow to walk on water and turn water to wine. Many people are enjoying the five course meals from the pastor's sermons but are not willing to learn how to make the five course meals from scratch on their own, because if you know how to make it from scratch whenever you have a need you know exactly how to go about it.

CHAPTER TWENTY-FOUR
PRAYER

$$\rightleftarrows$$

"Men ought always to pray and not faint" (Luke 18:1)

"Pray without ceasing" (1 Thessalonians 5:17)

Prayer is a continual lifestyle and not an event only when trouble knocks, but an everyday mindset in life. Prayer is the channel through which we communicate with God. Jesus Christ said, "We ought always to pray and not faint," also the Bible says to pray without ceasing. Look it doesn't say: "pray when you have a problem," but it says, "pray without ceasing." That means prayer can be done over anything, anywhere, every day. Most people pray only when they face a challenge. It shouldn't just be so, you ought to be ready before the challenge so when the challenge comes you already have a strategy for it. What made Jesus Christ's ministry and life powerful is that He was a man of prayer, He prayed for everything, He asked His disciples to pray with Him for an hour, and some asked Him how to pray (Luke 11:1). They saw what prayer was doing in His life they wanted to learn how to pray so they can have the same result like Him.

Prayer is the way of life for the believer, you can't dodge prayer, at some point you will have to do some prayer and fasting, it is a path all of us have to take—nobody is exempt unless you are in the grave. But as long you are alive, prayer has to be part of your life. The Bible says the Holy Spirit can't speak of Himself, but what He hears, that shall He speak and receive from Jesus Christ and show you things to come (John 16:13-15), nothing just happens unless you work it. Don't mess with a person who knows how to pray, they can call fire and suspend the rain for three years, Joshua suspended the sun for 24 hours because he prayed (Joshua 10:12-15).

Job was restored what he lost because of prayer, he prayed for his friends and God blessed him greatly (Job 42:5-10). Jabez was greatly blessed because of prayer (1 Chronicles 4:9-10). Jesus Christ prayed when going to the cross (Matthew 26:36-37). The Apostle Paul's eyes were opened up, so he could be launched for ministry, the man of God prayed for him and he received his sight to win souls for the Kingdom (Acts 9:4-18). Whatever you do, learn to pray and fast, it will help you on your journey here on earth. Prayer will help you avoid falling into satan's trap, because you will grow to hear the voice of the Good Shepherd (Jesus Christ) and the voice of the stranger you will not obey or follow (John 10:1-5). Many times I almost fell into sin, but because of my prayer life, the Spirit of God warned me not to do it. There was a plot to kill me through witchcraft, there have been many, but every time the plan is made; God will open my spiritual eyes and tell me what to pray, and I will pray and confess I shall live and not die (Psalms 118:17) and much more with long life He satisfies me and shows me His salvation (Psalms 91:16) and seal it with the blood of Jesus Christ for life is in the blood (Leviticus 17:11) and praying in tongues, and proclaim the works of God and His protection over my life and what belongs to me.

Pray and ask God to give you that grace to be a person of prayer. God said He is looking for someone to stand in the gap and could not find one, in other words He is looking for an intercessor and can't see anyone who was praying, so He can intervene (Ezekiel 22:30). That is God speaking on the matter of prayer, that should tell you something—that God values prayer a lot. The Bible says when you pray in the Holy Spirit (tongues) you speak not to men but to God (1 Corinthians 14:2) and you are building your holy faith (Jude 20). Your faith can be built by prayer as well. The woman with the issue of blood was healed because of prayer (Luke 8:43-48), Lazarus was resurrected because of prayer (John 39-44), the man at the pool of Bethesda was made whole because of grace and prayer (John 5:4-9), the blind man received his sight because of prayer and faith (Luke 18:36-42), the man who was naked and possessed with demons was set free because of the authority of prayer. After that encounter he was set free, no one could recognize him, do you see what prayer does? It renews you and reinstates your identity in Jesus Christ. He was naked because of lack of prayer, but because of the authority in prayer, now he is clothed and in his right mind. I can feel the joy that family witnessed when their loved one is in his right mind because of the authority of prayer (Mark 5:2-16).

Jesus Christ's prayer life made impact on the disciples and they saw the end result what prayer can do. He sent His Word and healed them all. He prayed and exercised authority (Psalm 107:19-21). "The prayer of the righteous avail much," (James 5:16). Prayer requires you to believe what the scriptures say about the issue. Jesus Christ sent His disciples to go pray for someone, but they could not get the result they needed. They prayed, but it was not a prayer of faith. Later Jesus Christ was asked how come His disciples could not get it done, His response was that unbelief was the root of the problem, it was as simple as that (Matthew 17:14:-21). A prayer of faith will heal the sick and change the situation (James 5:15). Believe what you are praying about, don't make it a routine, but a lifestyle of impact. Don't take your prayer life lightly, it may cost you your destiny.

There was a man in the book of 2 Chronicles. His name was Asa and he consulted everyone except God. In other words, he refused to pray and because of that, God let him die (2 Chronicles 16:12-13). I felt sorry for the man, he refused to believe and talk to God, so God let him die. Don't let your life end up like Asa, take charge of your prayer life. How do I know that we communicate with God through prayer? It says in the book of Daniel, "When you prayed the first day I have heard you," (Daniel 10:12-13). Your confidence in prayer comes from the scriptures and from the confidence you have in God and His Word. When you know God hears you, nothing else can stop you. The Bible says, "This is the confidence we have in Him," (1 John 5:14-15), "That He hears us and we shall have what we ask according to His Word," not according to people's opinions, but according to God's Word. Cast not away your confidence, it comes with great rewards (Hebrews 10:35). Stay confident and stay in prayer and watch God do His part.

To any pastor, bishop, or five-fold minister; if you are not spending enough time with God—I mean quality time—and your members are spending more time with God in prayer, fasting, and study of the Word; don't be surprised when God speaks to them more than you. Jesus Christ spent more time with God than His disciples did, that's why He knew more than them and was able to teach them as well. You will not see anywhere in the Bible that Jesus' disciples went to the mountain to pray. If they went somewhere it's because Jesus Christ took them with Him. Never underestimate what prayer can do; it will change your life and the lives of people you come in contact with, that's what the life of prayer does.

Prayer Point

Father God Yahweh, you said ask and it shall be given to you. Yahweh, give me strength and the zeal to be a person of prayer. Empower me to live a life of prayer to the glory of your name, give me the grace to partake on this lifestyle as a believer of prayer and fasting. I thank you Father for granting me my request, in the name of Jesus Christ I pray. Amen

Now start to pray daily for 20 minutes and keep increasing it. Get into a prayer group at your church and learn the art of prayer, if the disciples have to ask Jesus Christ to teach them to pray (Luke 11:1-4), that should tell you something. It must be very important.

I heard the man of God once say: every failure in life is a prayer failure. Think about it for a minute. When you fail to pray, you have failed to inquire the result from God. The fight with the devil and principalities can only be dealt with through prayer in the name of Jesus Christ not through wishing. I heard a man say, "A closed mouth can't be fed," that is deep. If you can't pray you will not get the result you need. God said, "Open your mouth [wide] and I will fill it," (Psalms 81:10). You may not know what to pray, but when you open your mouth—God will give you what to pray. Prayer is the way of life for the believer.

CHAPTER TWENTY-FIVE
I'M IN THE GAME

⇄

Are you a player on a team or are you a bench warmer? Even though you may be a bench warmer, you are still part of the team; but you will not be cheered on like those who are making impact. Not everybody who is claiming to be a professing believer, acts on their faith as they claim to believe. I find that hard to believe, because the Bible says, "You shall know the tree by its fruit (Matthew 7:16-25), after 5, 10, 15, even 20 years in the church, what fruit have you produced? I did not write this—God did. God is really challenging a lot of saints on this, after many years in the church God expect us to display fruits, because God is interested in fruit and not in non-productive numbers. That question really caused me to examine my Christian life and walk. He said you shall know the tree by its fruit, the fruit shows how good the tree is. You will be surprised how many babes are in the church and the length they have been going to church, it's choking to know. They are people who "do" church as usual, yet have refused to grow or challenge the Word of God. The drug dealers can't take over our communities when we are professing soldiers for Jesus Christ!

The difference between the playing roster and those who are on the bench is that those who are on the roster, practice a lot to be better every time, but the bench warmers are not as consistent as those on the roster. Those on the roster make less mistakes so that it doesn't cost the team a lot, but those who are on the bench are there because their actions caused the team to lose because of not being efficient in their contribution, not enough wisdom of the game, or lack of quickness to make a play that will allow the team to move ahead. Based on the amount of believers that come to fellowship we should not have the gangs or prostitutes invading our communities. Now remember we wrestle not against flesh and blood, but against principalities and ruler of darkness and over all the work of the enemy which is satan and his agents (Ephesians 6:12). Remember the devil comes to kill, steal, and destroy. The devil really comes to kill—look at the crime rate of children dying before their time, he surely wants to steal the children, look at how many children are not in school but are part of the gang now that their future is stolen from them, if they don't get divine intervention.

He surely wants to destroy, children locked up in jail their lives are in jeopardy all those things are the work of satan and a little bit of ignorance (John 10:10). As professing Christians all these should not be our portion, "Goodness and mercy shall follow you all the days of your life," (Psalm 23:6). What I have just mentioned is not good news at all—kill, steal and destroy—it's not good news at all.

We've got to bring change to our communities; when a crime does take place I see people protest against the outcome of the crime, but you need to understand, this is deeper than your physical protest... you need a spiritual protest. Our neighborhoods need to be dedicated to God and not to idols.

I heard a testimony of the great man of God in Nigeria named Benson Andrew Idahosa. An occult group wanted to hold a satanic meeting in his town and he heard about it, he went into spiritual madness, and the news invited him on national TV and this what he said, "The occult meeting will not take place, if it does; I am not a man of God," that's what he said on live TV, that is boldness and confidence in your God; do you know that the occult group cancelled their meeting and it never took place, this should tell you how much charge we have over the spiritual realm. We need to get together and fast, pray, and seek the face of God over our communities. Let's stop being comfortable over satan's abuse. Heaven has no violence, but your God promised you to live Heaven on earth.

You need to remind God of His promise (Isaiah 43:26). He said remind me of my promise and let's plead together. Remember, God did not forget His promise; He just wants you to know it, so you know what you are entitled to. Don't be offended if nobody wants to join forces with you, not everyone will be on your side. It ought to be that way, but unfortunately it's not, and that's ok. When Gideon went to war he wanted an entire army but God told him no. So he ended up winning the war with less than what the other camp had. The war on terror is not a war of natural weapon, it's a war of spiritual warfare. I wish our so called leaders in politics understood that. Not everyone that comes to church is for you. There are witches and wizards in the churches and wizards and witches are in our communities. Their job is to hinder the will of God manifesting on earth as it is Heaven. The Apostle Paul said he could have been doing God's work sooner but satan hindered him (1 Thessalonians 2:18). Thank God he got saved.

I hate to say this, but I truly hate it when people say "rest in peace." Look, you can have peace on earth not only when you die! I encourage every leader, pastor, and others to hold their members and themselves accountable to let the presence and the name of Jesus Christ reign in their cities, schools and communities. At the end of the day, every failure we witness in our communities is a spiritual failure. Not anything else. It's hard to hear, but it is the absolute truth. Train your members to be strong fighters in the spirit and in the Word of God.

Jesus Christ was outraged when the fig tree could not produce fruit, while it had the ability to do so. The tree was capable, but was not yielding increase, it was in its season to produce and Jesus Christ cursed it to the root (Matthew 21:18-20). You ought to be outraged in the spirit that you have to drive three miles to buy groceries because in your neighborhood everything is out of business.

You ought to be mad at dryness and poverty around you. Call those things that be not as though they were (Romans 4:17) call those good businesses in. It is your birthright to live well and not sweat.

God has promised us that a desolate city can become like the Garden of Eden (Ezekiel 36:35), this is a powerful promise. Eden is a place of no lack only abundance; "You are not a stranger," says the Word of God, "but a citizen of the Kingdom of God." (Ephesians 2:19). Demand what is yours: peace in your communities, good schools where prayer is allowed, good businesses and so forth. All that can be done it is a faith project and roster problem to handle; it's not a bench warmer project. Every city needs to have a group of intercessors "watch men" not just at the church. That's what Nehemiah did in order to rebuild the city that was destroyed (Nehemiah 4:6-9). With prayer you will quench all fiery darts of the wicked (Ephesians 6:16). Anything ungodly that manifests in the natural was not vetoed first in the spiritual realm, every fiery dart of satan manifests only because nobody interceded.

The military has a defense system that destroys missiles; the concept was conceived in the spirit then manifested in the natural all that you see in the natural have existed in the Spirit realm first. Nothing just happens like that, it is a process and we need to be sensitive to hear what is going on in the spirit then veto that evil plot and agenda with the prayer of faith.

CHAPTER TWENTY-SIX
RECLAIMING OUR COMMUNITIES FOR JESUS CHRIST

⇄

This is a spiritual principal: every city and community is control by an authority. The mayor of the city of Chicago can't rule over the mayor of the city of Oakbrook, even though they are in the same state. They have limit under certain jurisdiction. If the Mayor of Chicago is under attack in Oakbrook, Forest Park, or Lombard, as the leader and part of the authority of the American government he can call back up from any city and they will assist him. It is the same in the spiritual realm; a Pastor who has been ordained in the spirit realm over a certain jurisdiction has power to run out demons in that jurisdiction where the spiritual recognizes him, when you are out of jurisdiction without Heaven's consent and covering you are in trouble with the satanic forces that control that environment.

You are free to go anywhere but if attacked you have the right to defeat those demons because you did not start the fight they did. That's why Jesus Christ, before He went to any city, needed to get

Heaven's clearance first before He could go in and do wonders in that city like never before. He had to wait on Heaven's backing. If you are invited to another church to preach and you have Heaven's clearance, you can disturb the evil forces that control that city because in that moment you have the seal of heaven and God's protection to do this, says the Lord. You see in 1 Kings 19:15-17 God was instructing Elijah to place kings and prophets in their territory. In order to be protected, they needed to be in the place where the spiritual realm recognizes them.

The mistake that the men made in the book of Acts when they were attacked by demons (Acts 19:14-17) was that they were trying to operate on a ground that was not assigned to them, neither did they have jurisdiction over. I'm sure those demons knew Paul's spiritual sons because they were under his covering. Yet the demons said to them, "Paul I know, Jesus Christ, I know, but who are you?" Those demons recognized that Paul and Jesus Christ had the stamp of Heaven and were given authority in the spiritual real to operate on that ground. Those demons couldn't do them any harm but had to obey their command, whenever given to them because of the authority they had from the kingdom of Heaven

Many ministries are struggling because they are planted in the place where the spiritual realm does not recognize them. Many are struggling in ministry because the spirit realm does not know them as ruler of that territory. It is very important to be under the right covering. To withstand attacks, you need clearance to operate in authority. If you are operating under a wrong jurisdiction you are on your own, you need to ask God where He wants you to open a church, where you need to open a business, and where to live. When God assigns you somewhere He gives you protection.

When Jesus Christ was tempted by satan the Bible says in verse 11 of Matthew 4 that the angels came and ministered to Him (Matthew 4:1-11). He was assigned divine protection because of His calling and assignment. An ambassador of America in Iraq does not have the same security as the ambassador of America in Japan. Why? Because the threats are not the same, but still they receive protection based on their assigned environment so it is with Heaven.

When Jacob had to meet Esau, the Bible says the angels of God met him. Why? Because he was under a territory that was not assigned to him, so he had to be protected (Genesis 32:1-3). When Daniel was put in the lion's den, Daniel said, "My God has sent his angel, and has shut the lion's mouths, that they have not hurt me," (Daniel 6:22). The angels were assigned for his protection because he was out of his jurisdiction, he was at a place where the spiritual realm recognized that he was protected by Heaven and they could not touch him. We have become so dull in searching the mind of God in many things.

If every church is at the place where they need to be under spiritual clearance watch what will happen, the kingdom of darkness will be tormented with just the presence of the saints.

Satan does not plant his churches anywhere. He is very strategic. Those who leave one church from another because they were offended or by choice and expect to be protected, not so my dear. You need to get spiritual clearance before you move to another church. If you are assigned to another church, the spiritual realm will know you as a sheep of that shepherd and if you go where you are not a sheep of that shepherd you are on your own. The attack is for you to deal with because you don't have a covering. God will give you grace to get in order, but if disobedience continues, you are on your own. Seek God if the place you are is the place you need to be, otherwise you may have to relocate your church. Also as a member, if you have picked the location based on your desire but not under Heaven agenda you are on your own.

The ghetto needs you, the gentlemen's club needs to close because of your presence, crime needs to stop because of your mentorship program you have brought in the community, educate young men and young ladies, teaching them about self worth and teach them to grow and discover their purpose in life. We have failed God because we have failed to seek his mind and his plan. We need to get back from where we should be, every city, town and country should see the impact the church shall bring like never seen or heard before. We are the ones who should challenge satan because we are the only force that can dominate over him.

CHAPTER TWENTY-SEVEN
COVERING OVER THE COMMUNITY

$$\rightleftharpoons$$

Never underestimate the power of prayer and corporate prayer, one can chase a thousand and two can put ten thousand to flight (Deuteronomy 32:30). You have the angels at your service, when Jesus Christ was arrested on the way to the cross He said He could pray to the Father to give Him more than twelve legions of angels to back him up (Matthew 26:53). If Jesus Christ would have used angels, why not you. The angels of The Lord encamp around you and deliver you (Psalms 34:7). One angel can kill 185,000 people, so why be afraid of any evil threat instead being of good courage? That is the advice God gave Joshua; He told him I will be with you as I was with Moses (Joshua 1:5-7). God is with you too, just as He was with Moses, Gideon, Joshua, David against Goliath, and with Jesus Christ on the cross, so is He with you.

In any war there could be casualties but since you are with God, you will not suffer casualty, neither will your loved ones in the name of Jesus Christ.

Remember to live a life of repentance, holiness, and walking in your given authority that Jesus Christ gave you so satan doesn't have reason to accuse you before the Father. Satan is the accuser of the brethren, "He is cast down which accuse you before God day and night," (Revelation 12:10). When you fall, please repent quickly to stay cleansed by the precious blood of Jesus Christ and remove any stain satan may have used against you before God. The Bible is very precise about what we see in life, can you believe that some cities and lives are totally sold out to satan. If your city is sold to satan—through prayer, and supplication, and discernment God will reveal it to you.

Look what (Nahum 3:3-5) said about it.

> "The horseman lifted up both the bright and the glittering spear: and there is a multitude of slain, and a great number of carcases; and there is none end of their corpses; they stumble upon their corpses:
> "Because of the multitude of whoredoms of the well favoured harlot, the mistress of witchcrafts, that sell nations through her whoredoms, and families through her witchcrafts.
> "Behold, I am against thee, saith the Lord of host; and I will discover thy skirts upon thy face, and I will shew the nations thy nakedness, and the kingdoms thy shame."

See, a city can be sold to satan and someone can make a covenant with satan and allow him to be god over that city for their glory and power through blood sacrifices. Don't think murders that take place over a nation or city are random, they are evil sacrifices for dominion and power. A family or an individual can sell their lives and destiny to satan for a price. The price of fame, the price of power, some sell their birth right so they can be popular and famous for awhile and willing to enjoy a short moment of wealth in life, yet ultimately die.

The Bible puts it well—selling to satan to gain the whole world but loosing his soul that is what Jesus was referring to in Mark 8:36 where it says, "For the blessing of God make rich and adds no sorrow with it" (Proverbs 10:22). Many cities are under an evil pact and until that evil covenant is broken over the city, the community will still be under demonic attack and curse. Some cities have to declare a state-wide fast against any evil covenant and welcome the presence of God and make a covenant with Him, when this takes place you will see how much evil that state was under. Some church leaders and politicians will back out of such a decree because they could be the ones who are part of satan's camp to invoke evil from their evil altar for the city and country to remain in bondage. The Church has to take a lead or catastrophe will continue on our watch. The healing of the city and country are in repentance and seeking God's face. "If my people, which are called by my name, shall humble themselves, and pray, and seek my face, and turn from their wicked ways; then will I hear from Heaven, and I will forgive their sin, and will heal their land," (2 Chronicles 7:14).

Personal testimony

Many years ago, before I was saved, I was still in Africa and there was a man in my neighborhood who had the power to get women without any problem. One day my late friend and I asked him why he was so powerful. Women cried over him, they fight over him; they steal money from their Parents to give him, whatever he wanted they would get it for him regardless of the cost. Some had committed suicide over him, to make a long story short; he finally told us what was behind his power. He told us in secret, he went to see a woman in Zaire, now known as Democratic Republic of Congo, and that the woman gave him that power. So we gathered the info and we went to see her ourselves, he told us what to bring when we go there and so forth.

We bought perfume, cola, and so forth; but here comes the catch. All she wanted as pay was 25 cents and she was so beautiful, I have never seen an albino so beautiful, (it had nothing to do with her being an albino I'm just trying to describe her). The idea was that when she prayed over the perfume we brought she would put it inside her female part and you would have to sleep with her all night.

I have heard a song that says all night long, all night, but I have never heard or seen anyone sleep with a woman all night. No way, it's unheard off. I told my friend I would pass on this one; I didn't feel comfortable at all. But he went on and slept with her all night, when the morning came I saw him—he looked different in many ways and I asked him how was it and he said it was great, nothing but the best. I thank God I did not participate in that, I can tell you with sadness my friend died suddenly and until now people wonder how he died, but I know what did that, it was the covenant he made with that woman in the spirit by sleeping with her and sold his soul just to gain the popularity of women and to be the topic of the town. He did not have to die untimely death; it is unfortunate it went down that way.

Spiritual attack over Chicago

"And I sought for a man among them, that should make up the hedge, and stand in the gap before me for the land, that I should not destroy it: but I found none," (Ezekiel 22:30).

The killings in the City of Chicago are not random, but spiritual. I hope we understand that.

The problems in Chicago are very deep, Chicago is a blessed city but there were things done in the city that have invited in a spirit that is plaguing many places in the City of Chicago. Remember in the era of the Mob and the Mafia and so forth. Those days may be over with, but the damages done then are some of the root of what the City of Chicago is dealing with now.

A lot of organized crimes were done in those days and many innocent have lost their lives as well. Think about it with your inner spirit, what those organized crimes have done is they have unleashed the spirit of death and of murder in some parts of the City of Chicago, today if you trace where those killings are taking place I guaranteed you it will be the same path those organized crimes took place. The City of Chicago needs fasting and praying city wide, and ask God to cleanse that city because the blood of those people who were wrongly murdered, their blood is crying out in those places they were murdered. Any church in those territories where mass killings are taking place you need to pray and fast because you have to know how to deal with that spirit of death and murder, these spirits you will deal with are legions, they are not small powers, they are evil generals in place to balance evil accounts.

I don't know if Al-Capone and all those Mobs knew, what they were doing would eventually cause the city to be a ground for satan to claim territories within. The police or the national guard can be called anytime, but that won't solve the problem, the problem is not natural—it's spiritual, only the Higher power can deal with it not your imagination. What we need is city-wide repentance and crying out to God, then He will heal the land (2 Chronicles 7:14).

In Al-Capone's last days, he was tormented by a gentleman he killed, everyday at midnight he was visited by that gentleman who would torment him in his cell. Capone would cry out and scream and the guard would come and they would see nothing, nor hear anything but Capone could, he could not sleep at night because of the torment, I wonder why the gentleman would torment him only at midnight, why not in the day time? Could that be the time he took his last breath before he was murdered and that's why he was trying to remind Capone for his killing at that time.

Maybe the gentleman was not ready to die, maybe the gentleman told Capone the truth no one has ever told him and Capone did not like it and killed him, who knows. Capone spent his last days in torment by that gentleman until he died.

If the blood of this gentleman was going after his killer in the cell, how much the city that witnessed mass killings in various part of it, the blood of the innocent is crying for revenge, the spirit of death and murder needs to be cast out of the City of Chicago otherwise it will continue to plague it for a longtime. Every leader who cares about the state situation needs to participate in this fast and prayer. The devil needs to be put on notice, the churches in Chicago that understand spiritual and natural warfare need to work together and fight these giants of death and murder. Because some churches understand spiritual things but not natural things, they will need to understand both in order to overcome and fight battles that are necessary.

Take this account, this is scripture: when Jesus Christ went to the Gadarenes in Mark 5 and there was a spirit that was controlling that city and nobody could take authority over that spirit, that spirit was ruling the town, the spirit of torment feared nobody. The reason I say that is because as soon as Jesus Christ came out of the boat, that spirit went to meet him but it didn't know at the time who it went to challenge.

But when he saw Jesus Christ from afar off he went to worship Him because that spirit realized it wasn't whosoever, it was Jesus Christ the Messiah. He submitted to Him and Jesus Christ asked the spirit, "What is your name," and he said, "My name is Legion, for we are many." Jesus Christ had to cast them out and they have left town. There has never been an account of anybody being tormented in that town anymore. Why? Because the spirit was cast out. The city of Chicago is no different; the Legions have to be cast out in order to have peace in the city. Satan shouldn't and will not rule your city, if you believe in Jesus Christ and are serious in believing in him, your city shall disturb any evil powers trying to plant roots in your city. The Bible makes it clear in Psalms 24:1-10 that the earth is the Lord's and the fullness thereof, not satan but the Lord. As the church in authority it is our duty to manifest Jesus Christ over darkness and display the light of Him everywhere. The gospel is not in words only but in demonstration and power (1 Corinthians 4:20, 1 Peter 1:1-25).

Personal testimony

A few years ago, I was doing living assistance and I was sent to a house where I had to care for a middle aged lady. I went to work and the Lord did not tell me anything nor did the Holy Spirit. So I got to the place and I was told what to do and how they want things to be done in the home, to my surprise the husband of the lady came to me and started to tell me what is going on in their home. How they are tired of living there and are thinking to sell the house. Forty years ago, where their home was built, it used to be a farm land and on their property someone was killed there and every day since they have moved there they hear someone crying out for help, and sometimes they hear loud screams of the person seeking help. They have become so familiar with that man voice, so they did the researched about the property that's how they found out about it.

As the husband was talking to me about it and I started to ask him if he goes to church and his response was, he doesn't but he believes in God. Then I asked him do you know Jesus Christ and he said I believe in Him, then the dead man spoke and said he doesn't like me, I didn't hear it but the husband heard it and told me about it.

So I told him not to be weary and everything will be alright, I just finished my intercessory classes at Living Word Christian Center then and I was well equipped. I believed the sickness of his wife was due to what was done on that property, nobody in that city of Aurora could hear the scream of the dead man, nor their neighbors, only them alone. I asked him if I could pray for them and their home and he said go ahead, as I was praying and calling on the name of Jesus Christ and casting the spirit of death and torment to leave that property and never return in the name of Jesus Christ, I did not hear it but the husband told me the dead man cried out he hates me, he hates me and what did I come there for, and he said I am living and I am not coming back to this place. Since then they have not had any issue with the torment of that man, they have not heard the noise of someone cooking, the man calling some lady name, they have not heard someone taking a shower in their living room, peace has come to that home. That spirit of torment and control over that land knew I was with Jesus Christ and had no choice but to obey my authority and leave.

Why do I share this with you, not to sound spiritual, but just to let you know about the state of the crime we are witnessing in Chicago, that was only one man causing torment into one family and one house, so how about the mass killings that took place in the era of the Mobs and Al-Capone, those people are screaming, crying in those places of murder, just like I couldn't hear the voice of the dead man, many think those things aren't so because they don't hear or see anything. They think everything is alright. Prayer of authority cast that dead man out of that land, I felt for that family, I did put myself in their place, and as a born again believer I had to show them that God loves them and He cares.

CHAPTER TWENTY-EIGHT
POWER OF INTERCESSORY PRAYER

$$\rightleftarrows$$

Being an intercessor is a privilege and it is grace at another level. Because you see things that no one else sees and you engage in battles that no one will ever witness unless you are an intercessor. It is a beautiful thing and a privilege. But having such a mandate comes with big responsibilities. You are the one God is counting on as a missile sender against the kingdom of darkness, you are the forefront soldier God is depending on to manifest His plans on earth as it is in Heaven. It took intercessory prayer from Anna the prophetess who spent a good majority her life and time praying and fasting for the coming of the Messiah (Luke 2:37).

To be an intercessor you have to meet certain criteria. An intercessor has to be discrete and private, what you want to know in the spirit and natural is the same thing satan wants to know, because whenever it starts to get hard for him to achieve his goal, he wants to make a deal with you in order to cheat you on the promises of God. An intercessor needs to be slow to speak and quick to listen (James 1:19) so when you speak the Word it will not return void. It's by grace you obtain this, or you can ask God to grant you such a life style. You will never see a witch or wizard boast about doing things against the Kingdom of God, no, they remain discreet unless confronted by the saints.

A navy seal does not act however he wants—whether on a mission or not, he stays focused on the target. Not anyone can be a navy seal, you will have to obtain certain qualifications in order to be part of the task. Why? Because the goal is to assure accuracy when on the mission, it doesn't mean because you were on the other missions you will have to be on all of them, not so. When Gideon went to war and God told him to downsize the amount of soldiers he had, it sounded like a failure but it doesn't mean these soldiers who were not part of that mission were not good—not at all. They were good but not for that mission, because that mission required intensive action (Judges 7:4-7).

Can you fast for 21 days without fainting, can you sleep for 5 hours and pray all night, can you fast 3 days dry? All these are missions for certain warfare, these are keys in warfare and in many battles we engage in. Demons can't drive out demons only the saints can (Mark 3:24-26). As an intercessor, you've got to be a person who is consistently in the Word and praying in tongues, because praying in tongues gives you some revelation only the spirit of God can give you, and keep searching the mind of God and have sharp understanding of the seasons.

When Lazarus died, Jesus Christ was checking Heaven's calendar for clearance because there was a plot to kill Him, Heaven had to put angels in place before his departure to Lazarus tomb, but it took intercession to know what was going in the spirit realm based on the task that was before Him. Every country and city problem is an intercession problem, when you fail to intercede you have given satan the right to reign in that place, but when you intercede you serve satan notice to vacate. I have never seen a government without a defense team, intercessory is the defense team for the Kingdom of God against satan. If you are an intercessor take that seriously because God is counting greatly on you.

Do you know that satan's agents are very serious when it comes to fasting and doing contentions, they probably fast more than most believers.

They understand the power of fasting, Ahab and his wife Jezebel declared a fast against Naboth, you know Jezebel was an agent of satan, but she declared a fast, my question is to whom was she fasting to, later we see Naboth was dead and his goods were being taken by Ahab and Jezebel. They killed him through witchcraft and the Prophet Elijah was made aware of that by God (1 Kings 21:1-29).

There is a satanist and he was telling how they fast for certain missions, in order for him to be a satan top agent; he had to fast for 40 days, and he could only eat when it was dark around 9 pm, if he eats after the dawn he would be tortured and demoted, you see now how important fasting and prayer is.

I remember when I got the visa to come to America; I did not want to come empty handed so we went to a nearby African country to buy diamonds so I can sell them when I'm in the States. I went with my friend but before we went there we got a word from a friend of ours who went before us, that he was caught and put in jail, for he was accused for buying diamonds illegally, so on our way back we met this man. He had so much money, when I say he had money, he had it. So he started to talk to us and we told him where we came from and what happened, then he started to talk to us and told us some deep secret and reserved some, so my friend happened to go with his chauffeur I don't know if it was a set up or what.

He started to ask me if I wanted to become as rich as him and if I was really interested, and I said that I was. Little did I know there was a catch behind it. So he started to tell me how to go about it, he said if you really want it this is how it goes, you have few options and you choose what is best for you. He said the options are; you can sell your big toe in exchange for wealth, you can get women pregnant and have them to have an abortions, that will boost your wealth even greater because blood is more expensive than currency, and he said you can sell your sperm "never have kids again" or you can accept to have woman cycle every month, I have never seen a man having woman cycle in my life. I was so in shock to hear that and he went on by saying after few years you can sacrifice anyone in your family to reach a certain status in life, to the point anyone can envy you. Then I said how do you do these things and he said I will train you and he said the place where these altars and maison are located are in India, we will have to fly over there, nothing wrong with India, it just happens to be the place where they were conducting these things. I thank God my friend came back and we left it to that, I did not share those things with him because I knew he would be tempted to do it, because he always wanted to be like the man without knowing the man had sign a pact with satan.

I was not interested in it, because the words of my late father kept ringing in my ears; don't kill, don't steal and never sacrifice humans but fear God. When we left I told my friend to stay away from that man and later the man died in his sleep, by that time I was already in America two months prior to his death. Until now his family can't recount of his wealth, it all vanished, why? Because it was not of God. But this man was strong in fasting, he fasted a lot, but he made a lot of sacrifices as well. The Bible said in 1 Kings 21:25 that "Ahab did sell to work wickedness in the sight of the Lord," the key word is sell and in Nahum 3 (please read the entire chapter) it says cities were sold to witchcraft, destinies as well, that's why intercessory prayer is key. The only force that could deal with Ahab in his time was the church; no other force was able to stop him, but the church only.

Someone may wonder why all these things happened to me; well I did asked myself these questions. I thought I was not walking in the will of God, but like Apostle Paul said in 1 Corinthians 13:11 "When I was a child, I spake as a child, I understood as a child, I thought as a child: but when I became a man [mature Christian] I understood differently." Those things happened to me because satan was after my destiny and God allowed it so I know how this world functions. I like the response Jesus gave Pilate, He said you don't have power over me unless it was given to you from above (John 19:10-12). These things took place because God allowed me to see them. The devil is after your destiny; he went after Jesus Christ's destiny as well, he went after Adam destiny, and it is the plan of satan to fight the saints destinies. So when you see someone approach you about these things, I beg you to stay away from it, because it's not of God, it is evil and it will pave your way to hell if you partake of it. I believe the reason I came to America by that time, it is the way God has planned for me to escape the temptation (1 Corinthians 10:13). I was not born again then, who knows if I stayed longer what decision would have made, only God knows.

CHAPTER TWENTY-NINE
BE YOUR OWN MASTER OVER YOUR DESTINY

⇄

"And be renewed in the spirit of your mind; and that you put on the new man, which after God is created in righteousness and true holiness.

"Wherefore putting away lying, speak every man truth with his neighbor: for we are members one of another. Be you angry, and sin not: let not the sun go down upon your wrath:

"Neither give place to the devil." – Ephesians 4:23-27

"Let the mind of Jesus Christ be in you But we have the mind of Jesus Christ." – 1 Corinthians 2:16

Lazarus the beggar refused to be the master of his own destiny he allowed the rich man's wealth control his destiny while he had more to give than the rich man. He was the seed of Abraham and he did not want to tap onto the Abrahamic covenant right he had in order to be blessed. The saddest part is that Lazarus realized his greatness only when he was in Heaven; that is a tragedy (Luke 16:19-25). He could have enjoyed his days on earth like it was in Heaven. How many people today are still chasing those who have more money and privileges than they for a certain moment? The painful part is that when you are following them, you are being robbed of your destiny. If you are still eating crumbs you will never be full, but when you have the whole loaf of bread you have the option with whom you want to share it with. The only way you can control your destiny is if you become your own master, take charge of who you want to become and whom God has called you to be. Remember, you will have to answer to God one day about what you have done with what He gave you (Romans 14:12). No man will answer for you but yourself. There are never two people in a coffin, you came alone—you are surely leaving alone. So why won't you become the master of your life and destiny? Proverbs 22:7 says, "The rich rule over the poor, and the borrower is servant to the lender." When you are poor in your mind you are subject to being a servant, a rich mind is a ruling mind.

There is a trap in being in a posse, it robs your destiny. Many people would not have had to die untimely deaths, but did because they have allowed the wrong crowd rule their destiny and lives. Don't let drugs, women, men, poverty, or lack of forgiveness rob you from your destiny. Naomi's life was almost robbed, but I thank God for the presence of Ruth in her life, Naomi refused to be the same—she changed her name to bitter (Mara) (Ruth 1:20). Her name meant "Pleasant, delightful, beautiful" before, but tragedies caused her to change her point of view about life in general. Her husband died, her children died, and what else had happened to her we don't know about. The tragedies she witnessed were enough to change her point of view of her name and life (Ruth 1:1-20). She couldn't see anything pleasant or beautiful around her, all she could see was bitterness.

Be careful about judging a situation before hand, you don't know what God has in store, you may think it's over, but in the eyes of God it's not over, as long you are still alive and have hope for today, tomorrow, and later on—he that begun a good work in you shall finish it until the coming of Jesus Christ (Philippians 1:6). If Jesus Christ did not become the master of His life, He wouldn't have made it to the cross at all. Peter fought those who wanted to take Jesus Christ for a moment, the moment that changed the natural into the supernatural, the moment that saved humanity forever; and there comes a moment in life when you will have to take great decision and take ownership of your destiny, Jesus Christ had to rebuke Peter (John 18:10-11) and become the Master of what He came on earth for.

Wherever you are, make sure you are in the place that shapes you to become the master of your own destiny, do not make decision based on popularity, but make the decision based on your call. Nothing is easy, but in everything when you are willing you will enjoy the fruit of your labor (2 Timothy 2:6). Do not let anybody rob you from your greatness. Many great people are out there the problem is they have not become the master of their destiny, we are all created and born original but many are dying unfulfilled and as a carbon copy.

At some point in life you will have to confront reality or you will be robbed by fantasies. The reality of your dreams begins when you start to deal with reality, because people who hold on to excuses will never take ownership for their freedom. I would rather be a limping Israel than to be a struggling Jacob. Israel mastered his destiny and became richer than his uncle Laban and anyone in his family, because he made a decision to tap into his God given promise (Genesis 32:24-30). You shall be the head and not the tail, above only and not beneath (Deuteronomy 28:13) "...Blessed going out and blessed coming in," (Deuteronomy 28:2-8). "I'm the Lord your God which teaches you to profit and leads you in the way you should go," (Isaiah 48:17). God gives you witty inventions and creative ideas (Proverbs 8:12). You are a prospect of success and not failure, the only reason people fail is because they don't master what they own or want to achieve. Adam did not master the Garden of Eden, if he took ownership of it, he wouldn't have given it to Satan.

You can't please everybody when you are the master of your destiny. Adam fell because he wanted to please Eve, he had the power to rebuke her proposal, but he failed to master his destiny and came short of his God given duty—now he is a servant while he was created to be the master (Genesis 3:1-15), he is working hard now to eat and live while it was catered to him before. That's what happens when you fail to master what you ought to master (Genesis 3:17-19). Many people who are in jail are there because of the lack of mastering their lives, some are wrongly accused, but those are unique cases. Many knew, "If I do this I will end up there," but they did not master their lives to avoid that path. "There is a way that seem right to a man, but the end thereof is death," (Proverbs 14:12). There is an end to everything. Which end do you prefer, the one that says *"...good and faithful servant"* (Matthew 25:23) or the one that says "...go away from me I did not know you" (Matthew 7:22-23), because you failed to master your destiny and life.

Become the master of your prayer life, your finances, your marriage, your children's orientation, and your calling. Learn to seek God on your own; one day manna will stop coming from those you look up to for provision (Joshua 5:12), so learn to start fasting without your Pastor telling you what to do. Be in charge of your destiny. When people don't master their destiny they shy away from the challenge and prefer to go back in bondage instead of thriving to overcome the challenge. When the children of Israel heard the evil report of what the scouts saw in the land, they didn't see themselves as an overcomer. Be careful what you heed; false information can cause you to fear. God has done all these miracles for them, He destroyed nations for them why now fear. They decided to make a captain so they can return to Egypt (Numbers 14:3-4), didn't Egypt give them hard times? Instead of facing the challenge they prefer to go back to bondage.

Beware of people who prefer the old days and refuse to face the challenge; they can cause you not to master your destiny. Why look back? Lot's wife looked back and became a pillar of salt

(Genesis 19:26). If Joshua and Caleb did not take charge and master their destiny the children of Israel would still be in bondage, but they took charge and believed God and encouraged the rest to do the same, while the ten so called leaders gave the evil report that caused the camp to go into a fear for tomorrow. Do not be intimidated by any size—anything that seems large can shrink before your face if you take charge of it (Numbers 13:17-33). The cobra seems to appear larger when he is fighting the Mongoose but after a while the Mongoose become larger than the cobra, the difference is the fighting technic, whatever you can fight, it will lose power over you, but whatever you run from will always control you and dominate you until it is dealt with. Israel (Jacob) couldn't be at peace until he made peace with Esau (Genesis 33:9-11), but he had to become a master of his life in order to make that step and to be at peace with Esau after he stole his blessing and birthright (Genesis 27:30-36).

If Apostle Paul did not become the master of his life, he would have returned back to persecute Christians (Acts 9:13), but he was transformed by the encounter he had with Jesus Christ and became the master of his destiny and calling (Acts 9:4-19), the servant is not greater than his master (John 13:16). Jesus Christ said, "What you have given me I have lost none," (John 18:9). In other words everyone you gave me; I'm the Master of their being and I have not lost any because I'm not letting the wolf destroy them while I'm their shepherd, even Jesus Christ had to report to the Father about mastering his destiny. Beware of people who keep giving you whatever you need but never encourage you to launch out. Jesus

Christ encouraged Peter to launch out into the deep, "Think big Peter," in other words, "and let down your nets for a draught," let down your guards and use what God has placed in your hands and life.

Don't let your experience hold you back. Peter listened to Jesus Christ and he became the master of his destiny. He became a fisher of men (Luke 5:1-10), those people who don't encourage you will rob you from your destiny if you don't wake up quick. "Cursed is the man that puts his hope in men," (Jeremiah 17:5). Put your trust in God and become the master of your destiny and life by trusting in God. Isaiah almost missed entering into his destiny because he was so focused on King Uzziah, it took Uzziah's death in order for him to encounter the presence of The Lord. So if Uzziah did not die, Isaiah would still be blind spiritually because he focused on him instead of on God (Isaiah 6:1-9).

Personal testimony

I grew up in an upper class family, my Dad was a successful business man in Africa Congo; he was well known and achieved a lot in life. He took care of his family and his children; that can be burdensome. He took care of his nephews, nieces, brothers, sisters and friends. When I came to America that mindset was in me, I was looking at to my elder brother to do the same for me. But when I got born again and I was praying and God told me, Whenever God calls me by my name I know He wants to tell me something profound so He said, "Archange you are hindering yourself," I asked God what He meant, He said, "you have made your brother to be your god instead of me."

I said, "God what do you mean by that," He said, "When you have a need you go to him for provision, it's not his duty to provide for you it is my duty to do that because I have created you and not him; doesn't My Word say 'My God shall supply all your needs'" (Philippians 4:19). That encounter changed my view for my destiny, I started to depend on God for everything. See, my Dad thought he was doing his brothers, sisters, nieces, nephews and people around him service but instead he did them disservice. Many of those people died without mastering their destiny and that is a tragedy. Depend on God, make Him your sole provider and you will never be disappointed.

The power of right thinking

It is a curse to put your hope in men, I refuse to be cursed. I want to be blessed beyond measure by trusting in God (Jeremiah 17:7). Teach me how to fish so I can be a good fisher as well, but if you don't engage me, what then. Joseph did not become the prime minister of Egypt by a random act, it was destined to be, nobody could deny that, but the most important part for him was to become who he became, because he mastered his destiny and thinking, he took charge and refused to let the environment he was in decide his fate. He stood his ground in prison and out of prison, he had discipline that was abnormal, he was joyful and optimistic as nothing had happened to him, he was in jail falsely accused and still happy. When he saw the butler and the baker unhappy he could have said we are all in prison it's not a place to be happy any ways, but that was not his concern because of the power of right thinking he knew worry would not solve a thing but faith in God would (Genesis 40:4-8). When you master your destiny and thinking, what distracts others doesn't bother you any more, your focus is on the result and not on abortion of dreams and visions. Because he mastered his destiny, the pit had no choice but let him go in the place which he was destined to be, the place of affluence and influence.

What you think is what you become, as a man thinks, so is he (Proverbs 23:7). Your thinking has a lot to do with what you become, so when your thinking is transformed your life has no choice but to be transformed as well. You are what you eat, you digest what you eat. No one has set a limit on you but you, God said, "As far as you can see," (Genesis 15:5). How far can you see? Your spiritual eyesight will determine where you are going. Anyone who has achieved anything in life, is because they have seen it before hand and believed it, your actions display the level of your belief, you will not act beyond your level of belief, someone will not dare move into a $1 million home without any worries when they have based their income as their only source, but will not have any issue to believe God for a $800 rent, why? Because they don't believe it is possible to obtain that $ 1 Million level of living, it is obtainable if you get organized and build up your faith, same process but two different ways of thinking and believing. I have heard a Prophetic decree by the Prophet of God, he said, "God can make you a millionaire in a month," that could be hard to swallow for some, but it's a declaration of faith and you have to change your thinking to receive it in order to believe such a decree.

The Prophet Elijah said during the famine in his time he released a Prophetic decree he said tomorrow it will be plenty and it will be cheap, and someone said unless God open the windows of Heaven there is no way (2 Kings 7:18), on one side he is right, but you can't limit God, the Prophet was quoting Malachi 3:10 he was decreeing the word of faith, he had the right to change the situation in that town as the seer of the Almighty God, his saying sounded foolish but it was a declaration of creation, he called for resources from the unseen by standing on the Bible Scripture in Malachi that says God will open the windows of Heaven, the Prophet was talking about the supernatural, and the Prophet Elijah responded to the man by saying you will see it but will not partake of it, wow. His mind just robbed him from receiving what God was about to do, all he had to say was amen, and I receive it and stand on the Word.

The Word of God and the promises of God are yes and amen (2 Corinthians 1:20), also it says God will do nothing unless He reveals the secret to the Prophet his servant (Amos 3:7). He missed his breakthrough because of his mind set. It's true when they say lose everything but never lose your mind, the mind is a bad thing to waste, but the memory of the just is blessed (Proverbs 10:7). I have the mind of Jesus Christ (1 Corinthians 2:16). Meditate on this scripture, it is the scripture that stands against memory lost.

Peter almost missed his breakthrough, because of his mindset he couldn't cease the moment that would change his business and the fishing business forever. Jesus Christ told him to launch out into the deep and let down his net for a catch, Peter being a professional fisher man, knew you don't fish in the day time, but he also knew you don't question God when He tells you what to do, because whatever God tells you—just do it. Mary told His disciples, "Whatever He tells you just do it," (John 2:5). See the demand of God does not make sense, it makes faith. It should align with your thinking and your faith in Him.

Then Peter obeyed after that, the Bible said he caught net breaking loads of fishes, heavy loads; to the point he had to call for back up because it was too heavy for the boat to carry. Then when his mind lined up with the miracle, he realized his mind needed to be renewed to thinking big, when he realized that then he came to Jesus Christ, and said I'm a sinful man, he is right and it is scripture, anything that isn't birthed of faith is sin.

He thought what he usually catches was the limit—until Jesus Christ came to show him that he could catch as much as he wants. All he had to do is change his thinking. After that experience Peter took in so many fish, he was transformed, Jesus Christ gave him the mandate to win souls now, but once his eyes opened, he had no more toil in fishing because he understood the power of right thinking has a lot to do with the outcome of his goals, his eyes of understanding we're enlighten (Ephesians 1:18).

What held back the man at the pool of Bethesda was not the people around him or his inability to get help, it was his thinking that held him back, everyone was jumping in and getting healed, he could have made friends so when the move of the angel take place they could help him get his healing or miracle. Forty years was he there, until grace stepped in, Jesus Christ came and made it easy for him and healed him on the spot, I heard a man of God say, if you are on your way to Mississippi and it's taking you forty years to get there, you are on the wrong road, sometimes we fail to examine the situation; examine yourself and see if there is any faith; examine why it's taking you so long to get where you want to get—after all these years. It could be your thinking, so change your thinking and embrace the victory you need.

See, when Jesus Christ put mud on the blind man's eyes and He asked him to go wash his eyes, He didn't hold his hand in order to go wash his eyes, but He told him to go wash your eyes while mud was still there. Couldn't he lead him so he doesn't stumble, but he is telling him to go wash up his eyes, and he asked him, "What do you see," his seeing had a lot to do with where he needs to go, if he can see opportunities, he will not be afraid; now mud represent re-creation, we were made out of clay which is mud (Genesis 1:26-27), so in order to restore his sight a prophetic step was needed.

Now don't try putting mud in somebody's eyes unless you know for sure the Holy Spirit told you to do that, God does not function by formula, but by strategies. That's why the devil missed the plan of the cross. He thought God was the God of formula. The things of God are spiritually discerned because they are foolish to mere man (1 Corinthians 2:14). Renew your thinking and you will be fine. The difference between a poor man and a rich man is their thinking, the rich invest and the poor spend. The rich produce and the poor consume, that is the difference between them without excluding the choices they freely make. One of the biggest and hardest deliverances in this life is the deliverance of the mind; today society is going backwards due to the way people think.

CHAPTER THIRTY
ATTENTION CRITICS: GOD IS MY FOCUS

⇄

"To subvert a man in his cause, the Lord approve not. Who is he that said, and it come to pass, when the Lord command it not?" (Lamentations 3:36-37)

In other words, God does not approve of your critics to succeed over you.

Never stop amazing your critics, Hollywood has an award called *the critics choice award* and it is given annually and actors win that award. Why, even though their movie is not the ideal for the low minded critics, but those who value the art, vote for the movie to be recognized. Don't let your critics pull you back, instead prove them wrong with your best act and effort that wows your worst critics.

Satan told Jesus Christ, "Why go on the cross; no one can take on the sins of the whole world." He criticized Jesus, yet Jesus proved him wrong by dying for our sins and resurrecting on the 3rd day,

That isn't all, the man that was on the right hand side of Jesus Christ on the cross, he told Jesus, "If you are the Son of God, why don't you free yourself ?" (Luke 23:38-44) That is the worst kind of criticism you can get—when you are in agony and feel alone, but Jesus Christ did not respond to his critic, he kept silence. Many times you don't need to respond to your critics, instead focus on your journey and destination.

Responses to critics create distraction that will involve debates that could steal your time and focus. You should only respond to those who value you and what you do. See how the other man that was on Jesus' left hand side said, "I know that you are the Son of God and when you go to Heaven prepare a place for me." And Jesus Christ responded to him by saying, "Your place in Heaven is guaranteed." (Luke 23:32-43; Mark 15:16-40) Jesus Christ said in John 13:16 that the servant is not greater than his Master.

What Jesus Christ suffered we will suffer likewise. Jesus Christ was criticized a lot, He healed on the Sabbath—here comes the critics. He ate with the sinners—here come the critics. He hung out with the tax collector and thief—here come the critics. He said the things He overcame and as He did, you will do also... even greater things (John 14:12). Jesus Christ did not respond to His critics because He knew who He was, and He had nothing to prove. He has proven many things already, so His response was not necessary. He had the opportunity to show off His power, but He restrained Himself.

Titus 3:9 says to avoid foolish questions. It's very hard to do that when you have power to prove your critics wrong, but the power was not in His response but in His restraint. The power was not because He was the Son of God; the power was in His discipline, because lack of discipline would have messed up the plan of the cross.

Lack of discipline can cause you to loose contracts that are dear to you, because you want to compete with the critics. Never compete with your critics—you are above them. Anyone who criticizes you when you are making impact, it's a clear sign they wish to be like you but they are not. So the only way to bring you to their level is through criticism. Remember you are in Jesus Christ and not in crisis. When you answer a silly question, you are as silly as the person who asked it (Titus 3:9). So try to avoid foolish questions, they are unprofitable and vain. The goal of your critics is to push you to embarrassment, but be wise not to fall into their trap. Do not let your foolishness be the food your critics need to pull you down. You've got to be confident in yourself and never give your critics room to prove their criticism are right.

CHAPTER THIRTY-ONE
MINISTRY

⇌

Ministry is very broad, you can be a door man and that can be your assigned ministry, you may be a cab driver and that can be your ministry, you can be a teacher at school that can be your ministry. God will send people your way to minister to people and lead them in the right place it's not necessary to have a building when you are in that sort of ministry. When you are called for such a ministry you are still under the presence of the shepherd which is the Pastor at your local church. One of the biggest mistakes people make when they get such connection they rush to open a church, while God did not assign them for a full time ministry but as a point of contact to be a dot that will connect those people to the ministry they were assigned to, but because of lack of understanding they act that way.

Everyone in ministry is called to make impact, the place many people fail in ministry is when they try to compare their ministry with others or they lose focus of what they are called for. Or they start to make the ministry all about them and not about Jesus Christ. Jesus Christ said it's not me who does the work but the Father in me, in other words my ministry means nothing if the Father is not involved in it or if He is not at the center of it (John 5:19), That is really deep, Jesus Christ understood that the Father is the reason of His ministry and not because He is doing miracles and people are praising Him, so He can make the ministry all about Him, not at all He gave honor to whom honor is due (Romans 13:7).

Many people in ministry suffer from low self-esteem and have entered the field with wounds that are not healed. They want to fill that void of low self esteem by being the focus and praise of the ministry, but you serve a God that does not suffer low self-esteem, God does not need your praise and worship to be God, He is God with praise or without praise, you are who you are without human praise or whatever the case may be. Give honor to whom honor is due. I love that song that says "Jesus be the center it's all about you…" That's right, it's all about Jesus Christ.

The church has so many rock star these days, let's not be distracted from doing the work, lest satan take advantage of you (2 Corinthians 2:11). Distraction will still your passion. Pastors are losing members and are still content, you have to be mad in the spirit when your members are dying untimely deaths—you ought to be outraged and seek the face of God—don't just do the funeral. The reason you are content is because you have been distracted and have lost your passion for the souls. Stop the attack if the wolf is amongst your sheep. It requires Jesus Christ being at the center in order to think that way, when Jesus Christ is at the center, His heart beat become yours and you start to hate what He hates and love what He Loves. See there is no such thing as a professional christian because your christian walk is always evolving. For example there was a need for drinks at a wedding, He turned water to wine in a few minutes when it takes years to make good wine, (John 2:7-11). He could have turned water to champagne if that was the need at the wedding (John 2:1-10) I doubt it if He didn't make few champagnes out of that water.

He puts clay in the eyes of the blind man when He could have only said, "Be healed," and He said, "Lazarus come forth..." while he stank being in the tomb four days, but by the power of His presence the smell vanished and his body rearranged itself at the sound of the voice of Jesus Christ (John 11:39,43-44). Make Him the center of your ministry, your life and your ministry will never remain the same. Today many men of god want to be popular for babysitting the church and forgetting about the real message, the message of salvation and the Kingdom they belong to. Teach people to grow in God and awake them from their level of ignorance to the level of righteousness and sin not because some have not the knowledge of God (1 Corinthians 15:34). Jesus Christ did not babysit the Pharisees; he told them the truth so they could break free from the bondage they were in. Are you encouraging people to go to hell, or you are encouraging people to go to Heaven, are you encouraging them to discover their identity in Jesus Christ or are you keeping them bound in tradition? Eli, Samuel's spiritual father, encouraged his children for leaving anyway, but when judgement came he suffered the consequences, because he did not correct his sons (1 Samuel 2:23-25).

In Congo Africa there is a saying, "Regardless of your years on earth, the ears can't be longer than the head," (I'm referring to human beings now.) It doesn't matter if you are grown in age— don't think your Parents can't correct you, as long it is in line with the word of God welcome the correction because it is for your good. Obey your elders in the Lord as long as it edifies (Ephesians 6:1).

CHAPTER THIRTY-TWO
THE POWER OF EVANGELISM

$\rightleftarrows$

"And he called into him the twelve, and began to send them forth by two and two; and gave them power over unclean spirits;

"And commanded them that they should take nothing for their journey, save a staff only; no scrip, no bread, no money in their purse: But be shod with sandals; and not put on two coats.

"And he said unto them, in what place so ever you enter into a house, there abide till you depart from that place. And whosoever shall not receive you, nor hear you, when you depart thence, shake off the dust under your feet for a testimony against them. Verily I say into you, it shall be more tolerable for Sodom and Gomorrha in the day of judgment, than for that city.

"And they went out, and preached that men should repent."
(Mark 6:7-12)

"And saying, repent you: for the Kingdom of heaven is at hand." (Matthew 3:2)

"I came not to call the righteous, but sinners to repentance." (Luke 5:32)

See, the repentance of the people and nations depend on evangelism. If you don't evangelize, how can people hear of the hope that you have? Christ in you the hope of glory. Colossians 1:27 and Ezekiel 22:30 say that I sought for a man to stand in the gap, but he could not find any. As it says in the book of James 5:16 "The prayer of the righteous avail much."

Also Romans 10:14 says, "How then shall they call on him in whom they have not believed," The world today is suffering because they don't know who to call when they are in trouble, people go to psychics because they don't know who to call and who to go to, I thank God for the ministry of Billy Graham, Bill Winston, Creflo Dollar, Oral Roberts, Kenneth Hagin, Reinhard Bonnke, Kenneth Copeland, Joyce Meyers and so forth, they have saved many people that were on life support ready to enter hell, but God has used them to usher those souls to Heaven. Numbers 11:1-2 says that when people sinned and the wrath of God took place, it took Moses' prayer in order for God to shut down the fire. If Moses did not pray, the fire would have continued but because he took charge and acted on it with prayer the fire was stopped. When you pray you can place a death sentence on the issue or let it continue if you fail to pray (James 5:17-18).

It is God's will that none perish (1Timothy 2:3-4). It pains God when a soul does not make it to Heaven. It says that Heaven rejoices when a soul get saved (Luke 15:10). This should tell you how important it is to evangelize. You are led by the Spirit to do wonders (Romans 8:14). I love the passage where Jesus Christ is about to be crucified and he is spending the last few moment with his disciples before going on the cross, one of the disciple of Jesus Christ asked him, "How is it you will manifest into us (John 14:19-31), and not unto the world (John 14:22)." Well He can't because the world doesn't know Him because they are not born again, He will only manifest to those who are born again and the born again will display Jesus Christ in the power of evangelism and the power of the Holy Spirit, in and out of the church.

Evangelism is not only at church, but in our communities, cities and countries, the angels do not evangelize only people can. If angels can evangelize why did God have to send Cornelius to Joppa so the man of God can minister to him (Acts 10:1-11), Jesus Christ evangelized a lot about the Kingdom, and demonstrated the power of the Kingdom of God with signs and wonders. The church is the only channel that God is counting on to win souls and if the church fails to understand that; God will use a different strategy to win souls. Let's stop having fashion shows in the pulpit and in the pews, let's do the work. Jesus Christ said in Mark 3:3 my brothers and sisters are those who are doing the will of God and Proverbs 11:30 says everybody ought to win lost souls. The Bible says it takes wisdom to win souls, for he that win souls is wise, and in all you do get understanding (Proverbs 4:7); if you are not winning lost souls you need to ask yourself this question: why you are not out there winning souls? Once you understand that, then you will value why you need an evangelism team in your church, because understanding and wisdom is key to achieve great result in winning and keeping souls in your church and in the Kingdom.

CHAPTER THIRTY-THREE
I'M PROTECTED

⇄

God is the best protector ever, man may protect you—but their protection is in vain. The Bible says, "Except the Lord build the house, they labour in vain that build it: except the Lord keep the city, the watchman wake but in vain," (Psalms 127:1).

King David said, "For you have been a shelter for me, and a strong tower from the enemy." (Psalms 61:3)

It's okay to have the police around; it's okay to have an army and other securities. But if those who are protecting you have hope in themselves and not in God they are protecting you in vain, because their own strength can fail, but when the hope is in God, your strength increases. The role of the government is to protect their citizens and not oppress them. Jesus Christ came for our protection against the kingdom of darkness. Read what the Bible says here about the duty of government:

"For unto us a child is born, unto us a Son is given: and the Government shall be upon His Shoulder: and His Name shall be called Wonderful, Counsellor, The Mighty God, The Everlasting Father, The Prince of Peace. Of the increase of His Government and Peace there shall be no end, upon the throne of David, and upon His Kingdom, to order it and to establish it with judgment and with justice from henceforth even forever. The zeal of the Lord of host will perform this." (Isaiah 9:6-7)

God has guaranteed you supernatural protection against what you see and what you can't see because your Government is there to protect you.

Those who are in the armed forces; or anybody else you need to know; you can't put your faith in your weapons and self, those things can fail but God who promised you protection will never fail, but when you are under the government of God and your faith is in Him to protect you and He will do just that. Your protection is as secure as the government you are from. The Kingdom of God is the only Kingdom that guarantees you a well protected destiny. Put your hope in God He promised to watch over you and keep you in safety. Stop fearing that something will happen to you. Nothing will harm you under the protection of God. As a born again Christian, you are the citizen of the Kingdom of God (Ephesians 2:19) since you have received Jesus Christ as your Lord and Savior, your protection is guaranteed.

CHAPTER THIRTY-FOUR
THANKSGIVING

⇄

Thanksgiving is the best education that God has given us, if you can't thank God now, when will you thank Him? (Psalms 6:5) For in death there is no remembrance of you: in the grave who shall give you thanks. You might as well start thanking God now in everything you do or face in life. "In everything give thanks: for this is the will of God in Christ Jesus concerning you," (1 Thessalonians 5:18).

Thanksgiving is for your benefit, because thanksgiving is a sign of gratitude, honor, and value. Many people just thank God when things are good while He said, "In everything…" that means good or bad you still have to give thanks. I remember when my license was suspended and I could not drive for a while I just got tired of spending money with lawyers fees and spending a lot of time off work while in the court house. One day under the hot sun of Chicago, I was tired of going to court, as I was walking back home under that sun I started to give God thanks for the situation even though it was not looking good, I could lose my job over this because of times I have been taking off and I'm losing money as well.

I set time to thank God for the situation, I was walking near the Joliet prison, and all sudden a car pulled over and asked me to get in the car, I gave it no thought I got in the car and he took off after few miles the man started to tell me I don't know why I have picked you up, I don't know why I'm doing this, I surely don't. Now I started to wonder what is wrong with this man, why is he saying that. I did not ask him to stop he stopped on his own so why is he saying that I don't know why I'm doing this. I thought I was being kidnapped then I asked him is everything ok, then he said I could lose my license over this, I said over what, then he said it's illegal to pick up anybody by the prison because it could be an imitate that broke out of prison, so I don't know why I did this. It's because of thanksgiving God sent me transportation that even caused the law of man to be in suspension to make my day joyful. I tell you I went back to court the next day and my case was dismissed, the money I did pay for fees were reimbursed, and the lawyers that took my money gave me my money back, why? Because I was able to open my mouth and Honor God with Thanksgiving. Thank Him for the breath of life, thank Him for the rent you were able to pay, thank Him that you were able to pay your car note, thank him for your health, job, your children, wife; husband and so forth. Thank Him that you had lunch, supper; give Him thanks that you got what to wear.

Nowadays, not many people have the lifestyle of thanksgiving. You went to work and came back home safe, while there is snow, while it's raining and you did not have an accident that is a thanksgiving moment. Your children went to school and came back without any bad news that is a thanksgiving moment. See when you give thanks to God you are saying I honor you, I adore and value you. When our children say thanks to us because they value us; we encourage our children to be thankful because we want them to be in the habit of being grateful. When thanksgiving is heart felt—it touches the one who receive it. Remember to be thankful to God from now on.

See many people's blessings and answers to prayer are suspended in the air because of lack of thanksgiving. Nothing would have been restored to me if I did not give a heartfelt thanksgiving to God. Jesus Christ gave thanks to God many times. For instance, when Jesus Christ fed the multitude He told them to sit; then He took the food and thanked God (Matthew 15:36-37). During the last supper He took the bread and gave thanks in front of His disciples (Luke 22:15-19). When He went to raise Lazarus of Bethany He said, "Father; I thank you that you have heard me," (John 11:39-41) that was thanksgiving after prayer. Be thankful now when you are in the grave you can't give thanks.

CHAPTER THIRTY-FIVE
FOUNDATION

⇄

"If the foundations be destroyed, what can the righteous do?" (Psalms 11:3)

Many of the issues we face in the church come from home. The church teaches us the fundamentals of living according to the Word of God and those fundamentals need to be enforced in our foundation from home. Christians have been so naïve to some extent, thinking that because you have heard something from the pulpit that's it. And they just go along with it, this deception must be corrected. When your child is off the course of the Word of God you need to correct your child, when you don't apply correction, you make it harder for those who will supervise your child when you are absent. Also there are grown-ups who acts like children in the church, sleeping around with the church members, gossiping, and doing all sort of stuff. King David did not correct Absalom to the point he hated his brother and killed him because his other brother slept with his sister (2 Samuel 13:21-30).

Adonijah was not corrected by his father King David, and he grew up to disobey his fathers words and he died in disobedience because his father never corrected him to walk in obedience (1 Kings 1:4-9). Age does not guarantee maturity, maturity comes with education and being learned. Do not expect for your Pastor to re-educate your child for you, you are at church twice a week, what are you teaching yourself and your children the rest of the 5 days. That's why many issues we face with families in the church are the result of the foundation.

The Bible says, "Train up the child in the way he should go and when he gets old he will not depart from it," (Proverbs 22:6). Look what He did not say, it didn't say, "Pastor, train up your member's children." You, the parent, are the first trainer for your child and the church should just add more into the training. Chasten your child while there is hope, and let not your soul spare for his crying (Proverbs 19:18). Eli was the servant of God but the Bible calls Eli's sons Hophni and Phineas sons of Belial; they knew not the Lord (1 Samuel 2:12), these are the children of the prophet not just anybody but the prophet Eli. Belial means in Hebrew *worthless* when the Bible refers you as worthless you are worthless.

Their problem started from home, Eli was so focused in the church and did not enforced the fear, the joy, the privilege and responsibility for serving God to his children, he let them run wild and he did not correct them. They were doing what only the priest should do when it comes to sacrifice and so forth. They had a dirty lifestyle; they were sleeping around with church women and they did not obey and respect what their father told them and Eli did nothing about it (1 Samuel 2:22-25). Being a prophet and a man of God this should not have happened at all, many people think if I work it out with God my kids will be okay, not so.

Eli was so in love with the church and he forgot that the church starts from home, the proof is that two of his sons Hophni and Phinehas died during the war with the philistines, when he was told his sons died and he was not moved by it but as soon as the soldier mentioned the Ark of God is taken as well the Bible said Eli fell from off the seat backward and broke his neck and died. This is alarming the Ark of God can still be restored but you can't have your son's back once they die; the fact that his kids died should have been alarming to him but it wasn't (1 Samuel 10-18).

You've got to teach your kids so they can work it out with God, they have to repent on their own; they got to seek the face of God on their own—all that is in the foundation. Eli lost two son's in one day (1 Samuel 2:34) his children did not have to die an untimely death, but they did. They were not faithful to God, and God, raised up a priest from another house and that was Samuel the prophet (1 Samuel 2:35). Samuel did not cause any problem whatsoever where ever he was with Eli or in the church, why, because his mother Hannah taught him value from home. Hannah made sure her son Samuel was well equipped before she presented him to God and those values embodied his foundation.

I believe Hannah corrected Samuel very well when he was off course (Proverbs 3:11-12) the Bible says that God corrects whom He loves, if you spank your child the Bible said the correction will not kill your child (Proverbs 23:13). I do not get it when the government says if you spank your child it's abuse; listen your heavenly Government, says it is okay to spank your child—he will not die. You are the one who has to deal with the consequences not them, so do what is right to keep your child on track. Because whatever you don't deal with today could be your worse expense for tomorrow. I believe we are like in those days of Eli and Samuel where the word of God was so precious (1 Samuel 3:1) technology is here but it's not really here to better us when it comes to live a life of holiness and in the fear of the Lord, but instead it's teaching our children disobedience, perversion and selfishness, as parents we need to enforced those value of the word of God in the foundation of our children.

Remember your children's problem is a problem for someone else's child. If your child is raised right, someones child will not have to deal with the lack of correction and values they may lack. Remember you are as strong as your foundation; the church is as strong as the foundation we build in our children and ourselves. At home they listen to secular music instead of listening to gospel music. They imitate the world and wants to become like the world, the best culture is being the person of impact—a leader and not a follower. The Word of God makes it clear in the Bible that if the blind lead the blind, both will fall into a ditch (Matthew 15:14) the result of our children's failure has been them following the blind and that has been the source of failure in our children foundation and we got to teach them what is white and what is gold, not to be led by fantasy but become whom God has called you to be. You become what you are exposed to.

Joshua said, "For me and my house, we shall serve the Lord," (Joshua 24:15). Teaching our children the ways of God is the best gift and legacy we can give them, because they can gain and loose it all, but when you know the ways of God you are much stronger to overcome many obstacles, I hope we take this into consideration because the foundation of the house and of our children lays on the Word of God we put in them, because a tree is as strong as the root that supports it. Hagar who had Abraham baby, best known as the mother of Ishmael, came at a point where she couldn't care for her son and she was hopeless and lacked resources. The Bible said in (Genesis 21:16-17) that God heard the voice of the lad "Ishmael" and an angel was sent to provide for them, it was not the voice of the mother that touched God's heart it was the voice of the lad. Where did the lad learn that from? He learned it from his father Abraham how to call upon God, that scripture shows that God hears the cry and voice of our children, when we teach them the right way they can call God for us and God will answer, because there comes times in life when you don't feel like talking or praying but when your children know how God can prompt them to do so on your behalf so He can act for you.

CHAPTER THIRTY-SIX
BE A NAIL IN A SURE PLACE

$$\rightleftarrows$$

"I will fasten him as a nail in a sure place: and he shall be for a glorious throne to his father's house." (Isaiah 22:23)

In the church many people go from church to church—not because they are not happy where they are, but mostly because they are on the quest of a certain experience they want to re-live. See Elijah thought he was all that, he said, "I, even I only, remain a prophet of the Lord; but Baal's prophets are four hundred and fifty men," (1 Kings 18:22). So as he thought about being the only prophet, God could raise Him any other prophet anytime He wants, that doesn't mean Elijah can't be used by God any more, he can be still used by God, it may not be as often as he used to, but he is still the servant of God. It's not the miracle or performance that defines a ministry; it's the presence of God and the confirmation of your call. We have to understand it's not the pastor, the deacon, the prophet and so forth who does the miracle, it's God who does the miracle, if God doesn't act on it, no miracle will take place, now remember satan servants the magicians did the same miracle Moses was doing in Egypt but there came a time the serpent of Moses swallowed the serpent of all the magicians. This was the indication that Jesus Christ was going to destroy everything the world of darkness throws at you (Exodus 7:8-12). You have to understand that, do not be driven by miracles but be driven by the Spirit of God, because those who are led by the Spirit are the children of God (Romans 8:14).

Everything in the world is driven by the spirit, what you see in the natural is the manifestation of what existed in the spirit and now available in the natural, that's why we have a lot of occults, because they try to bootleg what God wants to release on earth and try to pervert it, just look at most music today, if you are not naked and not prideful you are not part of the culture; these things are in the spiritual world. What we see is the evidence; you've got to know who you are following. Make sure you seek God before you give yourself to someone who calls himself the man of God or anyone in general, don't be naive and don't just go with the flow, don't do that, that ignorance may cost you your destiny.

The Bible says"Believe not every spirit, but try the spirit whether they are of God," (1 John 1:1-4). Be faithful where God has planted you and be a blessing. There is a reward in being a faithful servant.

CHAPTER THIRTY-SEVEN
PRAY BEFORE YOU ATTEND CHURCH

$$\rightleftarrows$$

Do not rush into a place because it has the name church written on it. Don't just attend a church because someone gave you a bulletin, you have to pray about it and see if God wants you to attend. Unfortunately not many people are mature enough to follow those steps in order to find out if God want them to attend that church service and so forth. Today there are many churches and not every church that says Jesus Christ is Lord is a church of God (1 John 4:2-4). Satan is not stupid, he will use any trick he can to usher you under his evil web to trap you for his benefit, but if you pray God can warn you of the danger of attending certain churches. Remember you are a sheep to a certain flock it is your duty to seek the face of God in order to know which "flock" church you belong to.

Don't attend a church because your Parents attend there, it may not be the place God has intended for you, don't attend because your friends attend there, don't attend because of the popularity of the church, but attend because God revealed to you that is the place He wants you to go. The responsibility of your spiritual life depends on you and not on God, the Holy Spirit will direct you where to go, but you have to take the initiative to seek God to tell you where He wants you to be. Remember, be aware of your spiritual life, you have to preserve it at all cost.

Personal testimony

Let me tell you this, I have learned it in a big way. A friend of mine invited me to her house—she had received a servant of God to her place and she wanted me to come, I didn't go the first time when she invited me, but I went a few times after. This was my first time being exposed to a deliverance ministry, I was in a good church but I didn't do my spiritual homework before I attend; that servant gave words of knowledge, prophe-a-lie and so forth, none of the prophecies the servant gave came to pass.

The servant rarely gave her tithe and offering to that church, and the servant used the money given for personnel shopping and sometimes when we had meeting there was not enough money to pay for the room rented for the service, they will miss services and delegate the responsibility to someone who was not ordained as a pastor, a lot of spiritual aspect did not add up. See I knew my friend who invited me, I can't blame her for inviting me, but I should have done my own home work. This was a big lesson I have learned in dealing with ministries: not everything that shines is gold. I went in prayer and fasting seeking the face of God while still attending that so called "church," I sought the mind of God on that so called servant of God.

She came from another state I didn't know anybody who could give me the servant's bio, but I know God has that servant's bio, and God started to reveal to me things about the so called servant. That servant works with marine powers and is part of an evil altar, I had to run so fast from that place and the so called church closed after my departure, I have never fought like this in the spirit after the so called ministry was exposed. Spiritual warfare was intense, when I tell you this, believe me, spiritual dogs were sent to attack me in my sleep (spiritual dogs means the spirit of perversion sexual immorality) I would beat those dogs in my sleep so bad to the point they were bleeding and ran off, a tsunami was sent in my apartment to control my spiritual movement. After prayer I fell asleep and I saw the apartment I was living in with my wife and children was flooded and everywhere else in the building I stayed in, there was no water, but only in my apartment. I felt exhausted because the water was so high I almost drowned. Then I woke up stating to pray and called the Holy Spirit to cleanse my apartment then I invoked the fire of God like Elijah (1 Kings 18:37-39) to burn any evil mirror and evil sanitation deposited by that flood of water sent from satan agent. The so called servant came in my room at night and wanted to sleep with me, she was naked And suggesting me to engage in a sexual act with her then I woke I woke up and started to pray, she did this more than 5 times, she wanted to control my destiny by trying to make me her spiritual partner or husband through sexual intercourse in my sleep, and many things went on, but I thank God I was equipped to take on this fight and win. The grace of God covered me so well. I will never go to a church just because it's popular, that church grew so fast. But don't let that move you, seek God's face in honesty because it is at the expense of your soul, don't play with this, it's very important.

My deliverance took about a year, that doesn't mean God couldn't deliver me right away, it was a learning moment for me and God was there, even though I had to engage in constant spiritual fights one after another, but it was worth the experience. My name and destiny was being invoked for evil, I had signed some paper work as part of my contribution to that so called church, my signature was taken to an evil alter that I agreed to be part of them, ignorance is not an excuse. So they pressed on my signature before God saying I have signed the paper so it is valid, God knew I was innocent. I went in to help and not knowing it was at the expense of my soul, and the Holy Spirit gave me some prayer points to pray, I had one week of intense prayer and fasting waking up at 3am to pray, just as the Bible said, this kind could only be broken by prayer and fasting (Matthew 17:21).

I had to demand that list to be destroyed, the angels went in and took my name off that book, this wasn't easy saints; it was very serious. I would never wish this on anybody at all. I have learned my lesson, never again. She did miracles like everybody else, but they were demonic driven and not God driven. One of the worst things you can do in life, is to be spiritually asleep, many decisions you see manifested took place in the spiritual realm first. The violence you see in Chicago is taking place in the spirit realm first, before you see it manifest.

Point of reference

In life many people are drawn by what they see and what they hear, but many times people fail to examine the issue on their own. It's not the miracle that validates the call of the person, it's not the name of the church that validates if the presence of God is there, it's not the generosity of the Pastor that validates if he is called, because many people have been misled by those things and have been deceived, hurt, broken and have ended in the hands of wolves instead in the hands of the good shepherd.

What validates the church and the pastor, is the spirit of God and not by what they do. Satan and those that work with him imitate God, the Bible says satan himself is transformed into an angel of light (2 Corinthians 11:14). But regardless the length of the dawn the light always comes up but you don't have to go through that in order to learn, you can avoid those traps and setbacks. The Bible is the perfect blueprint that is at our disposable, when you you look in the Bible, everyone God has called as His servant, all have the point of reference. No one was called without a point of reference.

"Now these are the generations of the sons of Noah; Shem, Ham, and Japheth: and unto them were sons born after the flood. The sons of Japheth; Gomer, and Magog, and Madai, and Javan, and

Tubal, and Meshech, and Tiras. And the sons of Gomer; Ashkenaz, and Riphath, and Togarmah.

"By these were the isles of the Gentiles divided in their lands; every one after his tongue, after their families, in their nations. And the sons of Ham; Cush, and Mizraim, and Put, and Canaan. And the sons of Cush; Seba, and Havilah, and Sabtah, and Raamah, and Sabtecha: and the sons of Raamah; Sheba, and Dedan. And Cush begat Nimrod: he began to be a mighty one in the earth. He was a mighty hunter before the Lord: wherefore it is said, Even as Nimrod the mighty hunter before the Lord. And the beginning of his kingdom was Babel, and Erech, and Accad, and Calneh, in the land of Shinar. Out of that land went forth Asshur, and builded Nineveh, and the city Rehoboth, and Calah, And Resen between Nineveh and Calah: the same is a great city. And Mizraim begat Ludim, and Anamim, and Lehabim, and Naphtuhim, And Pathrusim, and Casluhim, (out of whom came the Philistines,) and Caphtorim. And Canaan begat Sidon his firstborn, and Heth, And the Jebusite, and the Amorite, and the Girgashite, And the Arvadite, and the Zemarite, and the Hamathite: and afterward were the families of the Canaanites spread abroad." (Genesis 10:1-3, 5-16, 18 KJV)

The Bible tells us about these points of references so we can trace where the person comes from and where they are going. A church or pastor who doesn't have a point of reference is in question. I do understand that the Holy Spirit can train you to be a Pastor and so forth, but the point of reference is needed to trace your journey, who is your spiritual father or mother, who do you report to, what do you believe in, and how you got where you are? All these things are important in the life of anybody. The only person who can't really be traced in the Bible is Melchizedek because there is no death of him nor his parents mentioned in the Bible:

"For this Melchisedec, king of Salem, priest of the most high God, who met Abraham returning from the slaughter of the kings, and blessed him; To whom also Abraham gave a tenth part of all; first being by interpretation King of righteousness, and after that also King of Salem, which is, King of peace; Without father, without mother, without descent, having neither beginning of days, nor end of life; but made like unto the Son of God; abideth a priest continually. Now consider how great this man was, unto whom even the patriarch Abraham gave the tenth of the spoils."   (Hebrews 7:1-4 KJV)

"Now these are the generations of Terah: Terah begat Abram, Nahor, and Haran; and Haran begat Lot. And Haran died before his father Terah in the land of his nativity, in Ur of the Chaldeans. And Abram and Nahor took them wives: the name of Abram's wife was Sarai; and the name of Nahor's wife, Milcah, the daughter of Haran, the father of Milcah, and the father of Iscah. But Sarai was barren; she had no child. And Terah took Abram his son, and Lot the son of Haran his son's son, and Sarai his daughter in law, his son Abram's wife; and they went forth with them from Ur of the Chaldeans, to go into the land of Canaan; and they came unto Haran, and dwelt there.

And the days of Terah were two hundred and five years: and Terah died in Haran." (Genesis 11:10-17, 19-25, 27-32 KJV)

Even Jesus Christ being as great as He is; can be traced from the beginning until to His birth and so forth (Isaiah 11:1-11) and (Matthew 1:1-18). You have to take these things in consideration before you join a church or let anyone lay hands on you, these things help you understand with what spirit they are working with, don't let those wonders you see lure you in, don't let the sound of the name of the church attract you, don't let the welcome you are receiving from that pastor distract you, don't let the marquis signs excite you, instead be led by the Spirit of God and do your own homework, because spiritual things are important to know because you are a Spirit and you can only deal with satan at the Spirit level and also God can only talk to you by your Spirit and not your flesh, because your flesh isn't the real you, but your Spirit is. Learn to be spiritually minded and be also spiritually learned, because your lack of knowing can cost you a lot.

The Bible declares that people are destroyed by lack of knowledge (Hosea 4:6), in other words, your destruction is linked to lack of knowing the truth. You are fully responsible for your spiritual growth. Therefore be mindful who you let speak to you and who you fellowship with. Never doubt your Spirit when you feel uncomfortable. While in a certain church, some people call it "instinct" but it could be that God does not want you in that place because of the shadow of evil that you can't detect with your natural eyes, when you sense something in your Spirit, it is a sign to ask God what is going on, because that feeling is never random; it is usually a sign that there is revelation that you need to know about. I tell you this because I was duped twice by false prophets who pretended to be people of God but were not at all, those feelings were there but I did not know how to go about it, my wife picked up on those things faster than I did, I thank God that I caught on. We have left those places because we have learned so much. The Holy Spirit has trained us and I have read books, listened to teachings that validate what the Holy Spirit showed me, how to detect what is going on in the Spiritual realm and that's how I came to know these things.

You will know what the fruit of a tree will be only by observing the strength of its roots. Preaching and miracles aren't enough; you need to have the conviction of the Holy Spirit that the pastor and prophet is a servant of God and not an agent of lucifer. You are precious to God and He will protect you, so you do not fall to those wicked disguised agent of darkness.

Another thing is you need to be really watchful, when a certain pastor starts to shower you with gifts, those gifts are never free, they are there to build a control system, because when he sees the quality in you that you don't see in yourself he will try either to delay you for entering into your purpose through those gifts, or he will use you for his benefit and not for the benefit of the gospel.

You may ask why the gift is that bad, well not all of them are bad, when you have a strange feeling, that is your cue right there, it is your spirit man warning you about the trap behind it, the gift could be given to you in order to control you, it could be given to you in order to feel guilty whenever you are asked to do something for the pastor or the ministry, it could be when it's time for you to leave whenever you feel unsatisfied in order to delay your departure because of guilt of what you were given while you were there. The Bible says in Exodus 23:8 that the gift blinds the wise, and perverts the words of the righteous, because there are people it's better for you to struggle than take their gift because their gift will embarrass you when you don't feel right about the relationship you have with them any longer, or when God has told you to move on and that gift can cause you to be disobedient unless you are obedient to God and careless about the criticism that will come after it all. There are pastors and prophets like that, and unfortunately, I have met quite a few in my life. Those are the people who are messing up the name of God and causing the sheep to go back in the world so satan can have them. Their job is to covenant with you so they can close your Heaven and make it to brass instead of open Heaven. These false pastors or false prophets have made up their mind to serve satan and to delay the children of God's destiny by associating with them.

I was in a good church and I loved being there, but when was led to go to those churches, it was a different arena for me and it was quite an experience. When things happened to me I almost ran off from church, I said, "What is the point to believe anyone who claims to be a man of God." I had those thoughts and I came to God and cried out to Him and said, "Why did you let this happen to me, and He said I allowed you to see those things so you can warn others. At the time I was mad about it but now I count it a privilege, and He told me, "Everything that shines is not gold," and He said, "When a designer makes clothes many people may wear the same thing, but when the real designer shows up he can tell which outfit is the real McCoy and what is the bogus one." That was my first release of believing there are good men of God out there still and the other scripture that totally set me free is Romans 8:39, "For nothing can separate [me] from the Love of God," my God is bigger than these false pastors and prophets, my advice to you is stay connected to God and you will never be disappointed, weigh the Word you are taught and you shall be fine.

Prayer Point

Father God, open my eyes from any place that I shouldn't be. Father, take ignorance away from me and incline me to wisdom, to be at the right place, at the right time, with the right understanding. Father I pray that you give me wisdom and boldness to say no to those who want to blind my spiritual eyes with gifts.

I refuse to advance the kingdom of darkness through ignorance, instead open my eyes to see what you want me to see.

Father I thank you for loving me and for saving me for not falling victim into satan and his agents. Holy Spirit be my guide into all truth in the name of Jesus Christ I pray. Amen and Amen.

CHAPTER THIRTY-EIGHT
INTERCESSOR

⇄

I have never seen a government without an army, every government has a defensive agency, every church should have an intercessor department. Intercessors are the soldiers in the body of Jesus Christ, they are the defense against satan and his army. A church without an intercessor is a church that is missing out on Heaven's calendar. When the USA fought in Kuwait, the evangelist Billy Graham was brought into the White House to intercede and the USA won the war with no casualties. This should tell you something, when Israel went to war when Moses hands were up they won, but when his hands were down they were in trouble. When he interceded they won, but when he didn't they were in trouble (Exodus 17:11). One can chase a thousand (Deuteronomy 32:30) so ten or more can overcome a city. That is the power of prayer and in order to live a life of prayer we have to be serious with God

Every man or women of God ought to be a person of prayer and have the heart of a shepherd, because prayer is your communication channel with God. How can you hear God when you don't talk to Him? The Bible goes further by saying the Holy Spirit will not speak of Himself, what He hears, that shall He speak; this tells me the Holy Spirit will only give us revelation when we pray (speak to Him). Azusa Street was the result of people asking for the move of God in the secret place. Every business ought to have an intercessor it's very important. Joseph was put in the palace not just to be governor of Egypt, but he was the intercessor of the city as well, that's why Egypt economy was thriving because of Joseph prayers and relationship with God. It's not for nothing the Bible said God will do nothing unless he reveals it to his servant the prophet first, see intercessor are God's right hand, he wants to reveal them what is in his mind and what he wants to do. A city is as strong as the power of its intercessors. "When a strong man keeps his palace, his goods are in peace: But when a stronger than he shall come upon him, and overcome him, he will take from him all his armour wherein he trusted, and divide his spoils" (Luke 11:21-22) and I like what the book of Matthew 12:29 says, "Else how can one enter into a strong man's house, and spoil his goods, expect he first bind the strong man? And then he will spoil his house," So when there is no intercessor, satan has easy access to break a city, ministry, business, marriage, and so forth. God is limited to intervene in a city because of the intercessor, Abraham interceded for Lot in Sodom and he was spared because of his prayers, when a land is suffering of many things, the keys to restoration is hid in the intercessory prayer, anything that satan attacks can be restored when prayer is applied with faith (2 Chronicles 7:14).

The only reason satan does not want you to pray or to intercede is because he knows prayer is the key to your deliverance and the miracle you need. Prayer chains satan and prayer destroys what satan had planned in secret against you or a nation.

Don't let satan encourage you to procrastinate on your prayer life because he knows that prayer is weapon that dismantle him and his agencies.

CHAPTER THIRTY-NINE
REVELATION IS BETTER
THAN INFORMATION

⇌

The problem with any economic challenge or deficit, is not that there are not enough good economists, they are plenty of them. In the time of Joseph they had plenty of them as is now. But having information is not enough and it will not solve or change the situation of the economy, because it is beyond human understanding. Intellect is inferior to recreate the economy, it requires revelation knowledge to stay on top of the famine. The King had a dream but no one understood the dream, many in Wall Street understood the economic downfall but no one holds the revelation to rebound the economy, it takes revelation to thrive in any famine. Famine shall never affect a believer. It is a promise from God, He said in time of famine you shall be satisfied (Psalms 37:19) but it takes revelation to partake of this promise.

The devil is never after you as a person, he is always after your potential and the gift in you. Satan did not go after Adam as a person, he went after him and his authority, the potential and gift he possessed (Genesis 3:9-12). God trusted Adam to the point that He allowed him to name the animals and everything else (Genesis 2:20). Adam was made in the image of God, had the nature of God in him (Genesis 1:27), but he settled for less and his potential was corrupted. Be very vigilant when challenges rises and examine the issue before you arrive at a conclusion, because the devil is not a fool, he knows what he wants and he wants to get it from whomsoever is a threat to him. And tries to make them his servants. Adam had to sweat while he didn't have to (Genesis 3:17). He had the potential and gift to reign and be god over satan but he let satan rob him from his potential and gift. Because of the fall, he became a servant while he was created to be the master on earth (Genesis 1:26), that's why being born again is key, because Jesus Christ has brought us back to Eden and be on top of the world having rulership that Adam had in the garden, and now it is restored to us by Jesus Christ because he is the last Adam (1 Corinthians 15:45-47).

Now do not think the garden is a small place, not so. The garden represents the world, all 7 continents Africa, Antarctica, Asia, Australia, Europe, North America and South America, he was assigned to rule and govern all 7 continents by God (Genesis 2:15-17). We have that mandate in us because we carry Jesus Christ with us, because Jesus Christ lives in you and you live by the faith of the Son of God who gave Himself for us (Galatians 2:20) See, your own failure is not every Christian's failure, because repentance is personal not collective, that's why Jesus Christ came; so each one of us have to work his own salvation. Adam carried the potential for the whole world, but not the gift.

Jesus Christ has the potential and the gift of the whole world and only in Him can you launch out and through Him is your divine calling. It pains me when I see men or women going after each other, thinking the guy they are going after is too handsome and and the lady is too pretty and end up in regret and heart break. See, that person wasn't after the real you, they were after your potential and gift. That's why people feel broken when they seem violated at some point because they feel they have lost their potential through an action. When satan told Jesus Christ to turn stone to bread, he was testing his potential. What potential He has! He can re-create from nothing, when satan told Jesus Christ to jump from the mountain he was testing if Jesus Christ had the backing of Heaven by using the right scripture to make Him believe it was the voice of God while it was not (Psalms 91:11).

He told Jesus Christ to bow and worship him and he will give Him all the treasure of the world, that temptation was to test Jesus Christ's identity if He knew who he was, those are the temptations satan uses to tarnish your potential and gift (Matthew 4:5-11). He told Eve if you eat this fruit you will be like God, see he was testing Eve's identity (Genesis 3:4-7), if she knew who she was, she wouldn't have fallen for that because she was already like God (Genesis 3:13). She had the power to ignore satan and focus on her husband and share with her husband what satan told her that day, but she fell for the fruit. See, the fruit is something that seems appealing but has a bitter after-taste, how many people fall into something and regret it big time because at first they thought it to be the ideal thing, instead it was meant for your fall. Not everything that seems appealing is good for you.

That woman may seem the prettiest but may have bad morals to keep a husband; he may be a handsome man but have an infidelity issue which prevents him from being a wonderful and faithful husband. You need to discern these tricks, many people's gifts have been tarnished by these tricks satan uses because of lack of knowledge. Many have the gift of being a great leader, great business man, or great football player, but they are in prison or dead; they have the potential, but it is destroyed by their own mistakes or lack of knowledge because they have fallen into satan's trap, that's why it is important to memorize Psalms 91, it has all the protection and exit verses in it, the Lord shall deliver you from the snare of the fowler.

Jesus Christ's potential was to regain the title from satan, and his gift is the crucifixion. As the Bible puts it, "God so loved the world that he gave his only Son..." (John 3:16) That is the best gift the world or anyone could ever receive, no other gift in the world will ever compare to that. Any problem in the world can't be solved by information but by revelation only. There is a lot of information out there, the devil missed the cross because he has and function by, information only and that's all he has, only God can give you the revelation to overcome any situations. Revelation takes you from now to eternity. Revelation showed Joseph the seven years of famine was coming to prepare for it. The king had information of the dream which he forgot, but it took revelation to override time from the now to the future in order to manage days to come.

CHAPTER FORTY
SOLDIERS ON DUTY

⇄

You will never win any battles if you don't know which battle you are fighting. Some battles require fasting and prayer. Some battles require silence. Some battles require praise and worship. Some battles require prayer and thanksgiving. Know your battle and use the right technique.

In order to be a navy seal you have to meet certain qualification, and to be in the army you have to meet certain qualification. A doctor by title can't work in a venue that is not his, you may be a doctor in dentistry surgery, but you can't function as a doctor in caesarian (C-Section) unless you qualify for that office.

In ministry, it's very important to put people where they fit. Placement in ministry is no different than in business; put people where they feel comfortable and are enjoying what they do, because when people are in the right place you don't have to beg them or force them to fulfill their duty. They will work and not complain a bit unless they are disrespected and mistreated.

A joyful helper is a loving helper. When you love what you do, you enjoy it. A person who does not enjoy what they do, is in the wrong field or they don't have an idea what they are there for. Lack of understanding can create confusion, the Bible makes it very clear, "In all your getting, get understanding," (Proverbs 4:7) Lack of knowledge can destroy a person and cause problems for others.

When you enjoy what you do, competition is out of the equation, all you should be focused on is getting the job done and going to the next assignment. Competition of who will get the glory is not even their goal, they do it because it must be done for a cause, David said isn't there a cause? (1 Samuel 17:29) Understanding causes people to do things for the right cause, don't do anything for an attention. Paul said, "When I was like a child, I spoke like a child," (1 Corinthians 13:11). Ministry and helps ministry is not for kids—not in age but in maturity of the spirit and understanding. Nobody comes to help and babysit others at the same time. A child-like mindset holds people back and the progress of the mission. Do everything as unto the Lord and not as unto men. Men can't recompense you, but God alone, He sees everything. Because sometimes people can be selfish and ungrateful that's why you look up to God and not to men for your recompense, but God is just and faithful. So whatever you do, do it for God and not men.

It's very hard to manage people who suffer from low self-esteem, whatever you may tell them, it feels like you are talking about them. We serve a God who does not suffer from low self-esteem; He doesn't need our praise or worship to feel good about Himself nor does He need to display His Godship. He is God wether you praise Him or not because He knows who He is and we have to get to that level, we don't need people's praise or worship in order to feel good about ourselves, feel good with praise of men or without the praise.

The Bible says Jesus did not pay attention to the praises of men, because He knew their heart (John 2:24-25). One day they say, "Hosanna" (John 12:12-13), the next day they will say, "Crucify Him" (John 19:1-7) be confident in you and in your God, the only thing you need to be aware off, is that God is happy with you, and you are doing what you're supposed to do and in submission under the vision God has given your man or woman of God. God wants a "do it" people—not a complaining people. Through complaining and murmuring, they missed the promised land. God wants a "do it" generation like Joshua and Caleb, they did not just encourage the people, they knew who they were, they knew in whom they believed and they believed the impossible and acted on it. God wants action and not just talk. A soldier on duty is not the one who always has something to say, but he does have something to contribute. Be the change and the one that makes history with God.

CHAPTER FORTY-ONE
STILL IN THE PLAN OF GOD

⇄

"For I know the thoughts that I think toward you, said the Lord, thoughts of peace, and not of evil, to give you an expected end.

"Then shall you call upon me, and you shall go and pray into me, and I will harken into you.

"And you shall seek me, and find me, when you shall search me with all your heart." (Jeremiah 29:11-13)

God is a unique God. When I say God, I mean the God of Abraham, Isaac and Jacob. Anybody can say God, but you need to mention the name of who you are referring to. When God showed up to Moses He introduced Himself with a different name that no one else have ever heard or known. In order for anybody to respond to the request they needed to hear a name they know Him by. He said to Moses to tell them "I AM THAT I AM" sent you (Exodus 3:14) "I AM THAT I AM" is a powerful name and statement, in other words He is telling Moses to tell them, "The

God of your father's whom you have known in one dimension is the same God that can manifest in whatever dimension you need Him." If you are in bondage He is your Savior, if you are hungry He is the bread of life, if you are persecuted He is your Lawyer for Judgement, if you are broke He is the one who gives you power to get wealth, if you are hurt He is the comforter, that's the same God, that's why He wants you to know He is "I AM THAT I AM."

I have come across many parents and when we talk, they always say to me, "You are a good child, I wish my kids were like you." I can sense worry in them for their child, what they will become and so forth. What they do not know is that I was once the same child they have—probably worse. I did not become like this overnight, it was the prayers of my mother and sister that were sent to God to change me. Every night until I came to America and maybe after, they prayed for me because I caused them shame, I had stolen from my parents and my sisters, I had a master key from my parent's bedroom, I knew where the money was; I was a customer in their bank, it was self-service for me without remorse, at 5 years old I could drink half of the bottle of wine, many times I was found on the kitchen floor asleep holding a bottle of wine in my hands, at 7 years old I could smoke 5 cigarettes a day, my older brother smoked and he always bought a pack of cigarette, I was never forbidden to enter his room, so I took cigarettes from him to go smoke outside the house at a nearby Elementary school.

Eventually I was caught later on after long years of smoking, I was disciplined very well when I was caught; at 5 years old someone gave me juice mixed with beer and whisky to drink, and I drank it to the point I was drunk, then wound up in the family swimming pool floating, people wondered how come I did not drown, it is not a random act, God was preparing me for this moment to share this book and revelation with you.

What I went through does not make my parents to be the worse parents out there, even in the palace there can be turmoil; I tell you they were good parents. I had elders and friends in the neighborhood who liked sleeping with prostitutes, so they introduced me to it. I never paid a prostitute twice, when I slept with a prostitute the first time they always told me to come back for free, I asked them why, the response was always the same, they told me that I was appealing to them. I thought I was all that until I got saved. I did all that when I was 13 to 15 years old. The day of my birth was quite a scene, I was born feet first and there happened to be a doctor who came back from his training and happened to be in the delivery room he was the only doctor who knew how to do such delivery, no other doctor in the hospital knew how to do it on that day, it was a matter of life and death but God had a doctor in training just for my coming in this world, still in the plan.

When I was 12 years old one of my friend's sisters introduced me to sex and caused me to sleep with her, she was the first woman I have slept with, she was 16 years at the time and I was 12 years old, it was an awkward experience but the more she lured me to have sex with her the more I got intrigue in sleeping around, she is the one who showed me how to be a hooligan, my life changed since that first day I encountered the feeling of having sex with a woman; she introduced me to the yearning of sexual desire which I never knew or wanted to know at that age, she could have gotten pregnant, she knew all that while I didn't, I was too young to inquire of those things, I use to play with my friends at his house but that day I left wounded and confused, I told a few of my friends and they crowned me to be the man, because to sleep with a woman older than you at that time you got to be a sweet talker, and I told some adult and they applauded me for it, and some did not believe me.

At the time I didn't know it was called molestation because there was no word for it back then in "Africa Congo" maybe because it was not talked about in our society back then. Little did they know, but this act can cause a child's psychological process to be delayed because of the act that took place, eventually that's what happened to me and it caused me to become very quiet and less interested in going to school and learning, I started to steal from my Parents and Sisters in order to be valued and loved, seeking attention and to be heard in the wrong way. I was wounded and hurt and no one knew it but me and God.

My life took a sudden turn when she asked me to watch adult movies with her while sleeping with her at their home. I lost it; it was just too much to deal with at once. You know how wild those movies can get and at 12 years old to see things like that it was a lot. My parents had to move me from them to my Aunty's house because I was last in school, I had never passed a class after that, my Mom had to pay extra every year so I can attend summer classes in order to go to the next class because it was a shame to be in a private school and not pass, but little she knew I was broken and my only focus was sex because I wanted to relive those moments we had. Coming to America was the beginning of the change I truly needed, but when I got saved and God started to open my eyes I saw what they were after, they were after my destiny. I know that I'm fearfully and wonderfully made (Psalms 139:14) but that was just too much easy access to deal with, but I came to realize the spirit that was working behind them wanted to waste my life by deceiving me with sex and false praises.

No prostitute does the work for free, they do it because they want money why I am exempt it does not make sense. It was because of my destiny. I'm sharing my past with you so you know that I'm not perfect, but God is still using me in my imperfection. My past is not appealing at all but I tell you this because I'm not ashamed of the gospel of Jesus Christ: for it is the power of God unto salvation to everyone that believe (Romans 1:16), I'm a changed man because of the gospel, who would have thought that I can write a book, who would have thought that I can go to church, who would have thought I can pray and there is a testimony, it's by grace, still in the plan of God regardless the flaws. Since I got born again I have discovered a secret.

Many parents worry and spend money on the things their child will never use in life; material things and school programs that will never benefit the child, choosing majors that are not meant for the child and wasting money and energy. There is a way not to give up on your child, seek God for the plan God has for your child.

Look what God said to Jeremiah:

> "Before I formed you in your mother's belly I knew you; and before you came out of the womb I sanctified you, and ordained you a prophet into the nations." (Jeremiah 1:3).

Look what God said about John the Baptist:

> "For He shall be great in the sight of the Lord, and shall drink neither wine nor strong drink: and he shall be filled with the Holy Spirit, even from his mother's womb. And many of the children of Israel shall he turn to the Lord their God. And he shall go before him in the spirit and power of Elias, to turn the hearts of the fathers to the children, and the disobedient to the wisdom of the just; to make ready people prepared for the Lord ." (Luke 1:15-17).

This what God said about the birth of Jesus Christ:

> "And, behold, you shall conceive in your womb, and bring forth a son, and shall call his name Jesus. He shall be great, and shall be called the Son of the Highest and the Lord God shall give into him the throne of his father David: And he shall resign over the house of Jacob forever, and of his kingdom there shall be no end." (Luke 1:31-33).

You have read the personalities of three people, Jeremiah, John the Baptist, and Jesus Christ, God gave their parents the bio of what they shall become in life, my proposition is: When your children are born or even before they are born, ask God the bio of their lives so you can train them in the right way and place them in the right field based on the bio God gives you. God has the purpose for that child that is acting insane. You read about me, now I am the servant of God still in the plan of God. Your child regardless of the crazy way he is acting, your daughter regardless the way she is acting—seek God to give you their bio so you can channel your prayers and fasting in the right direction.

God has the bio of your child; and only God can give you the info that you need. It's never too late to find out what purpose God has for your child regardless of their age. If they find out what their purpose is, God may show mercy and extend their days. I challenge you to seek God and get your child involved as well if they are adult, go on this journey with them it will save you money for not investing in the wrong field or wrong career, still in the plan.

CHAPTER FORTY-TWO
THE CHURCH OF JESUS CHRIST ON THE MOVE

⇌

The church has to mature very fast and be in position. We are coming into a time where every answer anybody needs will come out of the church. The spirit of God will move mighty amongst the saints, those playing church may lose that opportunity because it will require maturity, leadership, anointing, loyalty, faithfulness, and a pure heart to walk in that greatness and blessings that are coming. The world will envy the church and those who are in it. Tradition will be of no effect in those days, everything you will need an answer for will require the Spirit of God to fix it. If you are ruled by tradition and not revelation, you will toil in those days.

Get ready now, because the church has been so ignorant in taking its place, now God is going to speed up the process so the church should be honored like it should. It is impossible for Jesus Christ to be the groom of the church and the church not to feel impact and shine and be the light that the lost and the world needs (Matthew

5:13-18). The spirit of God is about to manifest in a way that will require a personal relationship with God to feel that impact. The Holy Spirit will show us things to come and how to operate in the supernatural (John 14:26), the natural will become so hard to function in because satan has corrupted the natural and you will need the supernatural in order to be 20 steps ahead of satan. Anytime God wants to override an evil plot He always uses the supernatural. For us to be saved He applied the supernatural—a virgin shall birth the Messiah (Luke 1:28-31), for the children of Israel to be free from Egypt God had to use the supernatural by opening up the red sea (Exodus 14:27-31). In order for Peter to catch the load of fish Jesus Christ used the supernatural (Luke 5:4-9). We have come to the point whereby the supernatural is the way to communicate with God, therefore maturity in the Word of God and your relationship with Yahweh has to be developed and be intact.

Matthew 5:13 says we are the salt of the earth. The church is in charge to change the world and not for the world to change the church. You are in the world and not of the world. We are the ones God is counting on to change the world. We are the only hope the world has. Those who do the talk and also do the walk are the ones that will demonstrate the God in them. Those who are lukewarm, God will reject (Revelation 3:16). When you face challenges that will test your relationship with God, you will have to be courageous and let your nay be nay, and your yea be yea. It's getting serious. Because in these last days deception will be relevant like never before

We can't be living anyway—we can't be influenced by what is going on in the world. The world needs to be influenced by what the church is doing because at the name of Jesus Christ of Nazareth, every knee shall bow and every tongue shall confess that Jesus Christ of Nazareth is Lord (Romans 14:11). We have the signature from Jesus Christ of Nazareth to use His name for the advantage of the kingdom, it's not about us, but it's about Him alone. Alleluia. Praise God.

Can God trust you to represent Him where you go? Jesus Christ said the kingdom of God is within you, that means where ever you go you carry the kingdom with you (Luke 17:20-21), that tells me whosoever is born again and received Jesus Christ of Nazareth as your Lord and Savior, you have the kingdom in you. The reason people act inferior is because they don't know what kingdom they are from. They have not been taught, its lack of knowledge. You are an ambassador for Christ and you carry on you privileges that nobody can give you but God (2 Corinthians 5:20-21).

If you are not concerned about your spiritual life and your spiritual growth, you are in trouble. You will never grow spiritually if you are not willing to invest in your spiritual life. In life many times you've got to be your own motivator, you can't wait on people to motivate you, if they are gone what will you become? Therefore be your own motivator in your life. Every one of us shall "give account of himself to God," (Romans 14:12). Now and then you may need some motivation but do not let that be your only source of encouragement, you will be surprised how many people live solely on compliments in order to feel good about themselves, no compliment—no good day. But the Bible says David encouraged himself in the Lord (1 Samuel 23:16), what does it mean to encourage yourself in the Lord? It means being joyful even when all odds are against you—having assurance in whom you believe, that's what it means by encouraging yourself. The man who was sick of the palsy had friends that did not let anybody stop them—they opened up the roof so their friend can receive the healing (Luke 5:18-20) they encouraged themselves in the Lord against all odds for the miracle they were looking for. The blind man Bartimaeus did not have anybody to encourage him to cry out for healing but he heard about what Jesus was doing and when Jesus happened to pass by him, he took the initiative to ask for his healing he encourage himself even when the disciples told him to be quiet (Mark 10:46-52).

I believe the blind man's faith drew Jesus to pass by him because faith attracts God to do wonders in your life beyond human understand; he didn't let anybody shut him down. He encouraged himself in The Lord. How can you relate to God when you are not feeding at His level? It's not by might not by power said the Lord but by My Spirit. See it didn't say flesh and blood, but it said Spirit. God is a Spirit he that comes to Him must communicate with Him at a spiritual level and not flesh level (John 4:24). God has no confidence in the flesh (Philippians 3:3). The Word makes it clear by saying, "out of the flesh dwells no good things."

When Jesus Christ asked his disciples who do you say that I am and a few of them mentioned names, but Peter said a word that drew an attention in the ears of Jesus Christ, by saying you are

Jesus Christ son of the living God, and Jesus Christ replied by saying, "flesh and blood did not reveal this to you but my Father who is in heaven." (Matthew 16:13-18). It took a spiritual download to get that discernment. He was on a spiritual high to get that answer right there. I don't know how the setting was when Jesus Christ asked that question. Was it after prayer, was it a trivia question and so forth. I love to imagine hanging with Jesus Christ and a question like that comes up. It must have been a unique moment. I wonder if the rest of the disciples were jealous of Peter, because no one got it right but him. Even Jesus Christ said those who worship God must do it in the spirit and in honesty "truth." Your spirit is the candle of The Lord (Proverbs 20:27). Those who are led by the spirit are the sons of God (Romans 8:14). The natural man doesn't receive the things of God because they are spiritually discerned (1 Corinthians 2:14). Your spirit is more powerful than your flesh. Because out of flesh dwell no good things.

You can't become a better you if you are not spiritually healed. When I say spiritually healed I mean your relationship with Jesus Christ is good, when I mean good it includes your prayer and the time you give Him, you study the Word and keep growing, not easily offended, don't easily get upset, people pleaser and so forth that's what I mean spiritually healed.

Another thing that has become a norm in the church is the state of divorce. Divorce is and has never been the will of God (Mark 10:4-6), unless you are in abusive relationship where you are beaten, and so forth, but not to leave because you are lusting after someone else. When you got married you went before maybe yes, maybe not, but I'm sure you confessed to everyone that you have heard from a God that he or she is the one, so why don't you seeking God's face before you start thinking about divorce, you don't because you don't care and you want it your way and not God's way. Many have cursed themselves because of wanting it their way. Many have lost their soul mate because of the way he was acting. Then "ask" God and wait on Him to tell you what to do in order to save your marriage.

One thing that has been a big deception with saints is that they want to manage their marriage like they were not saved, bring the unsaved carnal ways into the new you having sex toys and adult movies at home, doesn't the Word of God say, "Casting away imaginations and every high thing exalting itself against the knowledge of God and bring every thought captive to the obedience of Jesus Christ." (2 Corinthians 10:5). All that perversion will cause you to imagine a vain thing, and cause you to be perverted. Many carnal businesses ought to be out of business by now. I mean evil business it's because the so called saints are the number one sponsors. Many profess to be believers but do not act like it, with the amount of those who profess to be believers the porn industry would be out of business, the sex toys would be out of business. Abortion clinics ought to be closing and so forth. In 2013 the porn industries made $6 Billion and this is a fact, in that $6 Billion include those who don't pay their tithes, those who pay their tithes but don't sponsor any project at their local church but have devoted themselves to build the kingdom of darkness by buying DVD's and sex toys without even knowing that they are the ones who are keeping the kingdom of darkness afloat. It includes the very saints that you know who buys movies from a click of a button in the comfort of their home, living a secret life, full of carnality without knowing they are caught in the net of their embarrassment and preventing them to enjoy the fullness of opportunities God has for them.

Personal testimony

Let me give you my brief testimony, I was about 2 years born again and I saw a porn store not far away from the church I attend, and I went in and the Holy Spirit convicted me before I went in but I ignored it, the conviction was strong but I gave it no attention, I was single then and went in. As I went in, I didn't feel good about myself and I came out of there quickly, the most terrible thing happened, my car was parked in front of the store and as I came out to leave my car wouldn't start, and fear kicked in if someone who knows me passes by and sees me, what would that person think and how do I represent God by being caught in such venue.

I started to pray in tongues asking God to forgive me, it took a while because I had to hide while I was talking to God, then I felt the release in me and I went back to my car and started the car and the car had no problem whatsoever to start, I made a decision that day I would never enter those places neither will I sponsor any of those venues. I'm saved now and I can't think like the world. I got to think like God thinks. I was not raised in church all my life but when I got born again and God started to teach me his ways, I had to learn and change quick, because I'm the light of the world also the righteous are as bold as a lion (Proverbs 28:11). I have to say no to things that do not glorify God, also you have to be bold to say no to that life style. It requires courage and love for God to walk in Him and reject what He does not like.. Jesus Christ said if you love me, obey my commandment.

The time of just being informed is not enough because information is limited to a certain extent, but revelation is advanced knowledge that can be revealed by the Spirit of God. The story of the gospel has not changed. The fundamental of the gospel has always been the same, seek those who are lost, broken and rejected. Jesus Christ did not come for the just but for the unjust, He did not come for the righteous but for the unrighteousness. The problem with church today is that we are number driven and not impact driven. God is not moved by numbers, but by impact. Is your ministry changing your community, is your ministry changing the lives of those who are under you and away from you? Is your ministry displaying God's power, goodness, and love throughout the world? Those are the things that are dear to God. When you focus on that, you are considered a ministry of impact.

CHAPTER FORTY-THREE
VISION

⇄

Vision is a good thing, but I'm talking about a different kind of vision than human sight. The vision that is beyond your natural eyes but what you can see with your spiritual eyes. God told Abraham, "As far as you can see that I will give to you," He was telling him to see beyond the natural. There was no evidence of children running around, but God gave him a hint, if you can number the sand, so shall your seed be, that was enough to challenge his thinking. The Bible said to write down a vision and make it plain (Habakkuk 2:2-3). The vision can be delayed but that doesn't mean it will not come pass, delayed is not denied. But the Word of God says wait for it, wait for the vision it surely will manifest. But while you wait you keep improving your vision not compromise it or shrink it, but stick to what is in the drawing board.

There is a reason why the prophet said write it down, because what you don't write down can be easily forgotten when the blessing comes in. I have known and met people who had great ideas, but when the provisions came in, their attention was directed somewhere else and did not fulfill their long dream. Why? Because they had no drawing board to rely on or to look up to what they wanted to accomplish. "Without a vision people perish," (Proverbs 29:18) and another version of the Bible said, "Without a vision people run wild." When you carry a vision, sometimes you will have to be alone on your way to manifest it.

Not many people may understand you at times, but that shouldn't change your vision. Don't let your vision be aborted by people who don't appreciate you. I love Joseph, he didn't let anyone abort his vision of who he was created to be, even through the tribulations and trials he faced, he still carried the vision and the dream that was alive in him. Because of his consistency he saw it come to pass. The reason you have that vision it's because God is counting on you to bring it to pass. One the saddest thing is that many of the greatest visionaries are in the grave, they have not manifested what is in them. I encourage you to work on your vision and put your faith in God and speak His Word over your drawing board and watch it come to pass.

Prayer Point

Father God, I thank you for the vision you have given me. Father, I trust in you to make it good. Holy Spirit lead me and strengthen me to manifest this vision that the Father have placed in me. Increase me with witty inventions and creative ideas. I will not die premature in the name of Jesus Christ of Nazareth. My vision will not be aborted in me and those who are working with me will never corrupt the vision you have placed in me. I call in loyal helpers from the north, from the south, from the west, and from the east.

My helpers will locate me and I will not miss them, in the name of Jesus Christ of Nazareth. Holy Spirit open my spiritual eyes wide that I won't be ignorant of satan's device, let me be attentive to the voice of the Holy Spirit and not the voice of my enemies or of satan and his camp. Angels go forth before me and fight for me against any delays programmed ahead of me. I thank you now Father for the provision and I receive this request by faith in the name of Jesus Christ of Nazareth.

Pray over that vision and see what it will become. Never lose hope when things don't go as planned. The prophet told his servant after many years of no rain, to go see if it was raining, and the servant came back and said there is no rain, the prophet told the servant to go back again, and he came back and told him there is no rain, he went back and forth few times then he came back and told the Prophet I see a small cloud, and the Prophet said I hear the sound of abundance of rain (1Kings 18:41-46), you may start small, but extend your vision to the bigger cloud and tune in your ears to the sound of abundance of rain, abundance of rain it means no lack so much provision extend your networking and keep thinking big. See rain fall on everybody, but not everybody understands the benefit of rain, rain refreshes the earth, and rejuvenate it. I love the reaction of the servant, he did not sound frustrated but was obedient to the command of the Prophet, you need people who will honor your gift and celebrate your vision. One negative word from the servant could have frustrated the Prophet and it would not have been good. But because they were in one mind things worked out without interception.

CHAPTER FORTY-FOUR
FAVOR

$$\rightleftarrows$$

"And the Lord said, I will destroy man whom I have created from the face of the earth; both man, and beast, and the creeping thing, and the fowls of the air; for it repent me that I have made them. But Noah found grace (Favor) in the eyes of the Lord."
(Genesis 6:7-8).

"And the child Samuel grew on, and was in favor both with the Lord, and also with men." (1 Samuel 2:26).

"And Jesus Christ increased in wisdom and stature, and in favor with God and man." (Luke 2:52).

Favor is everybody's desire, I don't know anyone in the Bible who has done great things without having favor with God and men. Even Jesus Christ needed favor with men and with God in order to function in dominion on the earth. Having favor with God is very important, it will cause you to speed into manifestation instead of delays, what was going to take you 10 years to do, favor with God will cause you to do it in 3 years, look at what Jesus Christ did in 3 years of His ministry, until now, we still feel the impact, why because of favor, look at the life of Joseph, his leadership in saving an entire nation from famine was due to the favor of God upon him, until now many become great leader and investor based on the life of Joseph and his leadership, based on what he did in Egypt. The Bible said, "Good understanding gives favor," (Proverbs 13:15). It was the favor of God that caused the Virgin Mary to be chosen to be the one to birth the Messiah (Jesus Christ) and look what the bible said Virgin Mary you are highly favored, the Lord is with you: blessed are you among women (Luke 1:28). It is favor that caused her to be chosen amongst all the women in town?

Whatever you are called to do in life, you need to seek the favor of God, because without the favor of God the project can take a long time to manifest. But with favor you do not toil because God talks to people on your behalf and open doors that will work to your advantage. From now on seek the favor of God in everything you do, favor in your finance that doors open that are never opened to anyone you may know, favor at place of work that God open doors that will land you in the position that will develop your calling, favor with men to be patient with you when you are trying to adapt to a certain way of doing things, favor with your children that God allows you to become a better parents and to connect you places where your children can be exposed to places of affluence and influence, because favor is necessary to make it to the top. Make it your daily mindset that you will confess and expect favor and find favor with God and men and having good understanding in the sight of God and man (Proverbs 3:4).

CHAPTER FORTY-FIVE
HAVE FAITH IN GOD, YOU WILL MAKE IT

⇄

"And Jesus answering said into them, have faith in God.

"For verily I say into you, that whosoever shall say into this mountain, be thou removed, and be cast into the sea; and shall not doubt in his heart, but shall believe that those things which he said shall come to pass; he shall have whatsoever he said.

"Therefore I say into you, what things so ever you desire, when you pray, believe that you receive them, and you shall have them." (Mark 11:22-24).

Everybody goes through challenges, you can't prevent a bird from flying over your head, but you can stop it building a nest in your hair. Problems are not bad, they help you become a better you and they help you recognize your better helper, God allows us to face problems because He has a solution for it. Many times you face problems it seems like God doesn't care, which is not true at all,

God cares a lot, but problems also remind us that God is the only help we have. The bible reminds us to "look up from whence comes my help, my help comes from the Lord," (Psalms 124:8). See, God is the only one who does not sleep, He that watches over you and Israel does not slumber. Since God does not slumber, that tells me He is awake for you anytime you need Him (Psalms 121:1-5), Jeremiah 33:3 said, "Call upon me and I will answer thee and show you things you did not know." See, in times of problems, God promised to show you the things you didn't know about. God said He will answer you, not abandon you. Have faith in God and you will make it. When I say have faith in God, it's not a one time thing, but in everything you do or face. When you decide to live such a life style it will help you grow from faith to faith (Romans 1:17).

There is a reason the Bible encourages us to build our faith before the flood, so when the flood comes we can stand. It's hard to build when the flood is present. Meditate on God's Word and memorize the Scripture in every area of life. Scriptures of healing; finances; long life; peace; strength; love; joy; protection; favor and blessing, so when the flood comes—you will be satisfied even in time of famine, because confession brings possessions. If Joseph did not prepare for those years of famine, it would have been a disaster during those times, but because he prepared, he was not faced by the drought in the land (Genesis 41:25-32).

What made him survive was his faith in God, not his intellect or information, but the revelation of the Word of God that he carried in him. The Bible said if God is for me, who then can be against me? (Romans 8:31). Whatever happens, don't quit or worry, instead have faith in God and you will make it. Think about our father of faith "Abraham" if he did quit believing in God, Isaac would not have come, but he believed God and God made sure Abraham saw the promise come to pass because he did not quit, but believed in God.

CHAPTER FORTY-SIX
YOU WERE NOT CREATED TO FAIL

⇄

"And such as do wickedly against the covenant shall he corrupt by flatteries: but the people that do know their God shall be strong, and do exploits." (Daniel 11:32)

In other words, you don't entertain what is against the covenant between you and your God, but the people who know their God; shall be strong and shall never give up.

Those who know their God shall do exploits, you were not created to fail. Failure is not in God's vocabulary. The angels will never answer you if the words you are using are not found in the Heavenly dictionary, failure is not one of them, so choose your words carefully in order to have good success. When you apply the Word of God by faith over a negative situation you will see the manifestation because that is the only Word Heaven's dictionary has and angels respond to. Failure is never your portion because you serve the God of no failure, everything He does has success.

He said in Joshua 1:8, "Every place the soul of your feet shall tread upon I will give it to you." So every place you go with God by your side you are supposed to win.

Many people loose it because they don't go with God, what I mean by that is they don't get a strategy and confirmation plan from God before they go on the mission. You need that confirmation so in case things go sour you can go back and remind God about what he has promised you and why the outcome was not as expected. When Joshua lost the battle even though he had the confirmation from God, So when he lost, he went back and reminded God what He had promised him: that they will win the battle, but they didn't, they lost, and God revealed to him why they lost, it was the sin of Achan that caused them to lose the battle, and he had to fix it right away because he knew he was not created to fail nor does the God he serves have failure in his vocabulary (Joshua 7:6-13).

So when you fail—challenge God. Know His mind on the matter don't just let it go like that. King David had to give his resume when he faced goliath, it wasn't for him to show what he has done, but to let them know that he is with the God who has no failure track record, he helped him kill a lion, he helped him kill a bear and this one is no different, what he helped me do then, he will help me do it here again and God gave him the strategy to fight, his strategy was foolish, but wise before God (1 Samuel 17:34-50). The things of God are foolish to mere men because they require discernment (1 Corinthians 2:14), look at the end result, you can't compare a sword to a sling shot, but when God is with you a sling shot becomes stronger than the sword. So when you face failure and you would like to know why it is so; inquire of God, and He will tell you. I pray that the eyes of your understanding be enlightened by the Holy Spirit (Ephesians 1:18). Remember you were not created to fail, but to succeed in every task that is kingdom driven.

CHAPTER FORTY-SEVEN
CALLED FOR IMPACT

⇌

Impact is the word for trail blazer, a mere man won't even think of impact as a way for life. It is your duty to leave an impact where people don't know your God, even around those who have never seen the power of God at another level.

Your length in ministry doesn't necessary mean you know it all or have seen enough, a new person in ministry can achieve more than those who have been in ministry before him. Jesus Christ was a new comer in ministry than those who were there before him, you have a Rabbi like Nicodemus who had been in the church for a very long time and was bound by the law and tradition and you have Jesus Christ introducing him to the reality of what he has been missing, many times we despise those who don't have a name in ministry and judge them based on the amount of the years they have been in ministry instead of having their spiritual bio from the Holy Spirit, that's why Jesus Christ had to challenge His disciples because not many believed in Him as the Son of God, and He asked them who do you think I am.

It wasn't a clever question but it was a reality check question. He has told them enough of who He is and now He wants to make sure if they have done their homework and he wanted to know who got the revelation from Heaven of His personality and calling (Matthew 16:13-17). They all gave their opinions based on what they have heard, but none was able to get it right except Peter. Jesus Christ had been in ministry shorter than those who spent their time in the Synagogues, but He did more than they could achieve, it's not because He was the Son of God, it's because He spent more time in the presence of God and was doing what they were not doing. He was fasting, setting alone time in the presence of God, and was meditating on the scriptures and manifesting what the Word of God said. So your years in ministry does not guaranty that you are better than others.

If the new comer is spending more time with God, of course he will give you revelations that you don't know about and God will use that person more because God is into productivity. Jesus Christ said there is time for everything, He said He has to work while it's day, that means the time is coming when it will be dark (John 9:4), in order words time is of essence I have to what is needful right now because I'm under mission, and when the harvest is ripe, but there are few labors (Luke 10:2), with all the ministers we have in world how could that be, we have few labors, because not all of them have the concept of winning souls, spending time with God, fasting, praying for the souls, it's business as usual for many of them, that's why God wants to raise up labors that understand His plan, laborers that love what He loves, to seek and save those who are lost (Luke 10:2). Growth in ministry depends on the time you spend in the Word and with God, it's not the years you've been in it. If that was the case, the Catholic Church would be far ahead in saving souls, because they have elders that have been in the church for a very longtime. If that was the case, the Pope will be unleashing some great prophecies and mysteries we have never seen or heard, because they select the Pope based on the maturity in ministry and their tradition, but that's not how God looks at it.

We have been conformed to that thinking, that ministry is based on age and experience. Experience is good to a certain extent, but not always. Your time with God will always give you experience that no one can give you. Jesus Christ showed us that, also King David showed us that, he spent a lot of times in the presence of God, in order to write the Psalms. You have to soak in the presence of God to get that revelation. It was not experience that helped King David kill Goliath, it was the amount of time he had spent in the presence of God. And it helped him gain confidence, because he knew when "I'm in the presence of God, I witness this and that, and I don't think the presence of God has left me, because God knows I love him so much and I know He will not fail me." Experience of men say put on an armor and carry a sword, but spending time in the presence of God challenged human experience by saying "I just need a sling-shot and five stones."

Those around King David questioned him because of the resume of Goliath, but when you spend time with God, you will outperform those who have been in ministry longer than you and even shame your critics because God is with you. King David was a young man then, but those around him were vets in the field, but King David taught them a lesson that day, whenever God calls you, He places on you the ability to overcome but the responsibility lays on you to make impact by covenanting with Him and walking in His ways.

CHAPTER FORTY-EIGHT
YOUR CALLING

⇄

Being called to serve God is great; it's an honor and privilege. There are a lot of people in ministry that are occupying offices they were not called for. Some were ordained because they could speak eloquently, some got ordained because they could quote the scriptures well, but that doesn't mean they were called to ministry. What is a calling, a calling is the ability to reign in what you were created for by God and by yourself.

Many complain of the attacks they encounter and crying out to God for help. Many are being attacked by reason of their ignorance, because they are occupying an office which the spirit realm does not recognize or have record of. Since they have not been called to that office, they do not have protection from Heaven, they do not have protection from Heaven. When Abraham was called by God, he was protected everywhere he went, when you are placed in your calling, protection is given to you, angels are assigned to you as a duty to protect you. But when you are in the office which you are not called for, the spiritual world does not recognize you and they can attack you because you don't have protection. Nobody could touch Abraham because God was with him.

Today we have many Eliabs because Samuel poured oil on the wrong vessel instead of David. You have to hear from God clearly before you go into ministry, because when you are in your post, provision is not an issue any more. Attacks in ministry are present but angels are assigned to protect you when you are in your office, it's like calling an ambassador and not giving him the secret service to guard him; it doesn't make sense.

When you are called, protection comes with it, I heard the man of God say; "do bread come with that." The man of God was giving an illustration that there was a lady who went to buy food from a fast food BBQ restaurant, when she was given the food and she opened it and noticed bread was not in the bag, and she had to ask the sales person, where's the bread, in her own words she said, "do bread come with this?" Yes wherever God has called you for, provision comes with that. Yes provision comes with that, protection comes with that; anointing comes with it. Like the lady did, you will have to do like her, you've got to claim your right, but you will have to tap into the kingdom benefits and services. When you are in your office as you are called, it is your right to have the backing of Heaven. When Jesus Christ was attacked on his way to the cross he said, I could call twelve legions of angels (Matthew 26:53), in other words I can call in Heaven to send me back up because I'm reigning in my calling and purpose.. When you are in your office you are never alone, people may leave you, but you are never alone because God is there for you to make sure your office functions properly. Heaven has a the largest registry of staff that is ready to be sent to assist you in your office.

When one quits, God will send another, why? Because God wants your office to function right; in the Shalom style. So make sure you examine your calling before you just say yes, hear from God that's what He called you for. It is by God's grace we don't have many casualties in ministry. But the time is coming when the structure in the offices is about to change. I pray that you get in the right office. The bigger your calling the bigger your protection, if you are called into the ministry of deliverance and prophecy, your protection is not the same as a deacon because you don't deal with the same thing while ministering. If you are into the ministry of healing, your protection is different than someone who is in the ministry of teaching of the Word. Don't be a Pastor when you are not called to Pastor but to intercede, don't be a teacher when you are called to be an Evangelist. Your office determined the type of Heavenly angels assigned to you.

So as you have read this examine your calling and be in the arena you were called for even when it's not popular, it's not popularity that called you, it's God who has a need of you that's why he has placed such calling on you. All you have to do is obey and serve and the rest will fall in place through your obedience.

CHAPTER FORTY-NINE
MINISTER OF MUSIC

⇄

"But now bring me a minstrel, and it came to pass, when the minstrel played, that the hand of the Lord came upon him [Elisha]" (2 Kings 3:15)

"And when he had consulted with the people, he appointed singers unto the Lord, and that should praise the beauty of holiness, as they went out before the army, and to say, praise the Lord; for his mercy endures forever.

"And when they began to sing and praise, the Lord set ambushments against the children of Ammon, Moab and mount Seir, which were come against Judah; and they were smitten" (2 Chronicles 20:21-22).

Music is a very important tool in the realm of the spirit and in the natural. God is the author of music and He has created it for a great cause and purpose. Music can heal, deliver and so forth, but you know whatever is used for the wrong purpose will not yield the fruit it should. Satan was the chief musician in Heaven; he understands music and the purpose of it. I heard a psalmist one day say that he was leading praise and worship and his spiritual eyes opened and he saw satan laughing, satan does not laugh at just anything, he laughs only at things that are supposed to make impact but used wrongly. The psalmist then asked God what that meant and God told him why satan was laughing. This is what God told him, "When you are praising or worshipping me you have to do it with all your heart and with authority in whom you believe." That assurance welcomes God's presence. Now think about it for a minute, it sound so simple but when you look at it in a different angle, it is profound what He said.

The psalmist is a minister who ushers the presence of God, your job as a minister of music is to open the Heavens for the congregation and make it easier for the man of God to minister with ease, because the path has been created for him in the spirit. Remember, you are a minister of music, that means what you do is a ministry. Now if the minister of music lives any way, fornicating, sleeping around, drinking, or living a life that isn't pleasing before God. You have just made the church you minister to a laughing ground for satan, the intercessors in that church will have to step in for the man of God and call in extra help in the spirit (if they have intercessors) otherwise it will be a lot of toiling while it wasn't mean to be. If you live such life: fornicating, and drinking just to name a few, let go of of that boyfriend, let go of that girlfriend, let go of porn, sex toys, masturbation and so forth It's better for you to step down because you are not living a life that is pleasing to God and deal with the issue before getting back in that position. The church needs fruit and not show, God wants people who are serious and honest with him, not those who wants to use the church as apron to shelter their sinful life.

Music breaks barriers and every instrument has a mission, all instruments don't sound the same for a reason. Look at the wall of Jericho (Joshua 6:1-27), God told them what to do based on the role of the instrument, and the instrument makes impact in the spirit when it is played by a clean person—otherwise it's only noise in the air (Joshua 6:20-21). The spirit realm recognizes when the person playing the instrument is a God fearing person, it recognizes when the person is clean. When I say clean, I am saying, not fornicating, smoking, sleeping around, etc. As a matter of fact you are welcoming evil spirits because you are releasing virtue based on what you carry. Your job is to make it easier for the man of God and not harder.

A minister of music has to be a person of prayer and fasting, your role is as important as the Pastor. You have to live a God fearing life; that will help you flow with the man of God and those you are working with. That is why you need to be in the Word, fasting and prayer as much as the Pastor does so you become twain in the spirit, because your role is very crucial in the church. There is music in Heaven that has not been released yet, there are lyrics in Heaven that have not been heard yet and there are melodies in Heaven that have not been heard yet, so far, the melodies we hear now have been recycled from secular music. And God wants you to download the score list of Heaven in your spirit, but it can only be birth through your spirit because you were wired by God to download it from His Spirit through fellowshipping with Him in secret.

Nobody can sing like you, nobody can play like you, and nobody can do what you do. Ask the Holy Spirit to teach you how to play and ask the Holy Spirit to teach you how to minister and sing. I tell you miracles will break forth in the House of God without the man of God laying hands on anybody, demons will flee on their own, witches and wizards will be converted to Christianity because of the sound of Heaven.

Your job is very important before the people of God, and the words you speak are meant to release those who are bound. Do you know that when you are singing you are releasing a decree over people under the sound of your voice, and you know that the Word of God remove burdens and destroy yokes (Matthew 11:28-30), in order to get results, it must be done in faith, because whatever that is not born of faith, is sin. Now be careful minister of music, because they are known to be prideful; remember the scripture said God resists the proud, you have to be humble at all costs. Satan was cast out of Heaven because of pride, and he wants to influence music and every minister of music with his character, that's why you need to be sharp in the spirit to discern evil traps in order to stay on top.

Pastors please I advise you to be bold when you discern your Minister of Music is living a dark life, even the member of your choir because they all form one body of Minister of Music, their role is inclusive so you got to put a stop whenever you discern something that is not Godly going on and cause that person to sit down while you are standing with that person in prayer for deliverance, because many pastors think because so and so have a beautiful voice if I take her out of the choir, the church will sink, it will sink if people are your source, but it will rise when God is at the center and you enforce his value towards his people. You're the leader and don't let someone else mislead others because you don't want to confront the truth by avoiding some of the work you will have to do in the mean while as the leader, your faith will be tested in that moment as well your heart of the shepherd will be tested without forgetting your privacy life, will you expose the person or you will keep it to self and let God prove himself over the matter. But you will have to put a stop to those things, it is necessary. This isn't here to make anyone feel bad, because the church has to be the light it should, and the best place to start is in the house of God and with the people of a God.

When King David played the harp, it was the way he played and the anointing that was on him that welcomed the presence of God in that place. Every time he played the harp, King Saul was made well (1 Samuel 16:22-23). It was not the instrument but the person that played the instrument, he lived the life that was pleasing to God; think about it, that was only one instrument that brought down the presence of God in that palace, if the bass player, the key board player, the drummer, and the worshippers have the same anointing can you imagine what will happen in the church. It will be like in 1 Kings 8:10-11, where the presence of God will be so strong in the house. You need to know that you have the mind of Jesus Christ (1 Corinthians 2:16) (Philippians 4:7). Whatever you do, do it as unto the Lord. God is holding you accountable for your position, in Heaven the angles are singing 24/7 in the presence of God, your only influence should be the Word of God and the Holy Spirit. You have in you what the world needs, so stop copying the world. Instead of you following the world, let the world follow you because you are operating in the spirit that created the whole world at the sound of words and authority. You have it in you, all you have to do is walking in the fullness of His presence.

CHAPTER FIFTY
PROTOCOL

⇄

God told the children of Israel, "Choose you today who you will serve," (Joshua 24:15-17). It was that the spiritual record to whom they belong to.

The Bible said the children of the world are wiser than the children of light (Luke 16:8), because people of the world apply a certain wisdom that works based on the spiritual laws. But they are limited to because certain revelation is hidden from them, but those who are born again have no limit and the only limit is you.

Don't confuse your title with your assignment, Jesus Christ had the title of the Son of God, Prince of Peace, and Rabbi, but His assignment was to die and save the whole world. You could have the title of the pastor or prophet but your assignment could be to erratic poverty where you are planted.

The spiritual realm understands protocol, and it honors protocol. When things are done in order, the spiritual recognizes it and honors it. Jesus Christ the Son of God born of the virgin by the spirit of God, even the demons understood that and honored that, the demon said, "Jesus Christ Son of the living God we know who you are..." (Mark 5:6-9). Demons do not honor what they don't recognize, when they honor it, it does mean something. They said "Paul I know, Jesus Christ I know but who are you," (Acts 19:15-16) (in other words we don't recognize you.) The spiritual didn't recognize those men's in the book of Acts as having such authority and power over them (demons).

Israel (Jacob) had to make peace with Esau not because he didn't have peace in life, but he wanted the spiritual realm to record it that all was well, so nothing can disturb him anymore as far as peace is concerned and his blessing, that gesture caused order in his life, the spiritual realm had to honor it. There came a time when God did not share his mind with Abraham not until Lot left, why? Because there was dishonor in the spirit realm, Lot's servants and Abraham's servants were in strife and the spiritual recorded it and honored it, as soon as Lot left God spoke to Abraham and gave him a new revelation for the future (Genesis 13:7-18). There are people who will never hear from God until they separate from certain relationships, careers, and friends.

Jeroboam did not have to die the way he did, the spiritual realm recorded his disobedience and it was ready to set him up for a tragedy if he didn't repent, that's why the life of repentance is good. He died at his own expense and the spiritual realm recorded Solomon as King. See, nobody said the blood of Jeroboam be on King Solomon, why? Because the spiritual realm did not recognize it as murder, but as act of disobedience and his blood was on himself.

When you are under Heaven's protocol nothing fazes you at all, there is no shortage in Heaven; we are part of a warehouse that does not run out. All inventions are stored in the library of Heaven and whatever you need Heaven will supply that need, just like on earth we have the library of congress where every earthy inventions are stored, so it is in Heaven. So whatever you need, Heaven has abundance in stock to supply that need. Many people are poor, it's not because God doesn't want to bless them, it's because they have not upgrading their thinking to be blessed by God and the spiritual realm hid opportunities from them because it has the record of them not believing God at His Word nor do they believe God is able. He is well able dear beloved, just believe and update your thinking, you will be amazed how it is good to live by the word of God and enjoying Heaven on earth but you will have to follow certain protocol and that protocol is crazy faith, believing God is able.

CHAPTER FIFTY-ONE
SPEAK THE WORD ONLY

⇄

Jesus Christ said, The Word that I speak to you they are spirit and life." (John 6:63). There is truth in the Word of God; the truth is the evidence of the Word spoken. Be healed and healing take place that is the truth, by his stripes you were healed (Isaiah 53:5) that is the final evidence of the word spoken of God. Jesus Christ prayed for the man servant and he was healed right away (Matthew 8:5-10), even though the servant was not near. The master of the servant did bear record of that. That encounter right there showed us that there is no distance in the spirit. The servant was not there but when spoken by faith it manifested from the distance, that is the gospel, not words only but evidence is there to prove the God kind of faith has no limit but have power to go distances and bring restoration.

The Word of God will never fall to the ground and it can't be bound (2Timothy 2:9). The Word of God justifies itself, God said He and His Word are one, so God makes sure His Word justifies

His identity. The Word of God does sanctify, and it is truth (John 17:14-18). The Word of God will never fail (Luke 1:37). The Word of God is the only word that can set you free from any spiritual and natural bondage. The Word of God restores you wherever you are broken or sick. Even God had to use the Word in order to create the light, the day, the beast and everything else. It took the Word to dry the Red Sea. The Word of God is the only force that can ever defeat satan, from now on—speak the Word of God only when things do not go right. Do you know that when you get to Heaven the only language you will speak over there is the word, because that's all Heaven has, it has it's own language. So why don't you start acting like you're in Heaven by speaking with authority the word of God just like you were in Heaven. For the word of God is not there to keep you bound but to set you free.

CHAPTER FIFTY-TWO
HONOR

⇄

Honor the Lord with your substance, and with the first fruit of all your increase (Proverbs 3:9).

Honor is very important in our lives, God loves honor, and everyone else does as well. Today we honor the wrong people, everyday my prayer is that I honor the right people. Some people honor those who abuse women, some honor those who steal, some honor those who disrespect the elders, and this is very crucial in our society these days. The reason many young people are living any way is because they don't know the value of honor, they honor the wrong people, they honor the words of rap music more than the word of their Parents, elders, or God. They honor the words of their friends than the words of their teacher in the class. Anywhere there is honor, there is order. It doesn't matter if you have a big house, big ministry, or even a good job that you have dishonor your elders and those who supposed to be honor. King David committed a sin by killing Uriah and when God sent Nathan the

Prophet to come correct King David, Nathan didn't come to King David with shouting and nagging, he honored King David by calling him by his Kingship title then proceed with the correction of God (2 Samuel 12:12-9).

Dishonor has caused many people to die untimely deaths, the Bible said, "Honor your father and mother so your days be long upon the land (earth)" (Exodus 20:12). It does not matter if your father or mother were not there for you that you have to cast them out, you still give them the honor they deserve, your dishonor does not disqualify them from being your parents, they are still your parents, you carry their DNA, regardless of what you do, they will always be your parents, elders, and so forth.

The new generation needs to be taught about honor, back in the day teenagers used to say yes ma'am and yes sir and so forth. But now people will rob the elderly instead of helping them even though when they see them struggle for help, that is an act of dishonor and not honor. When you honor the right people you are covered with blessings, because God loves those who honor the right people. People honor their friends, managers, boyfriend, or girlfriend with gifts that are so outrages but have never given their parents a gift so good to the point they were in awe, when is the last time you have honored your Parents? When was the last time you have honored those who have made impact in your life. Whatever you do from now on, honor the right people in life and in your life.

CHAPTER FIFTY-THREE
LOYALTY

⇄

"Many people profess their loyalty, but a faithful person – who can find?" (Proverbs 20:6 NET)

Most men will proclaim everyone his own goodness: but a faithful man who can find?

"A faithful person will have an abundance of blessings, but the one who hastens to gain riches will not go unpunished." (Proverbs 28:20 NET).

Many people are more loyal to men than to God and they wonder why they have to toil to make it in life. When God is your first love and you are loyal to Him nothing in life will ever faze you because you know the God whom you serve is alive and He is with you. Your redeemer lives, the one who did conquer the grave. Jesus has conquered all problems that will rise up in your life. The Bible makes it clear by saying when a man's way pleases God you are loyal to God no one will ever be your problem, because you know God will fight for you when the plot is against you. When a man's way pleases God He makes him at peace with his enemy (Proverbs 16:7). Joseph was loyal to God and he knew when he was tried this is what he said, what was meant for evil my God turned it to good (Genesis 50:20). He knew what it meant being loyal to God, and God will be loyal to him. He could have slept with his boss' wife but he said I will not sin against my God (Genesis 39:4-13) "Honor", in other words I will be loyal to my God. And God kept blessing him because of his loyalty to God.

Abraham won all his battles because he was loyal to God, the world had to pay him damages when they tried to take his wife (Genesis 13:1-2), God shut the womb of the women in the camp because they tried to mess with the one who is loyal to God (Genesis 12:14-20). Stay loyal to God and God will fight your battles, the battle is not yours but the Lord's (1 Chronicles 5:22). When your loyal to God don't pay attention to the haters, you remain still and knowing that, He is God and He will care of it for you. Be still and know that I'm God. Be still and I will show them that I'm your God. Now being loyal to God means making God as your only source and option unless He tells you otherwise. Being loyal is having faith in what God said; and trusting Him and not looking around. If God called you to where you are and things are not going the way you have planned, don't change your mind but you still believe God, Abraham believed God against hope when there is no hope, but believed in the promises of God. It was not easy for Abraham to walk in loyalty with God, but he believed God and Honored God in his life.

Abraham having a baby with Hagar was not disloyalty but a mistake, Job wife was disloyal because when her children died she did not seek God face, instead she encouraged her husband to curse God and die (Job 2:9). The situation of Job and his wife is like the situation of Adam and Eve, if Job obeyed his wife's evil counsel to curse God; his life would have been finished, but because he was loyal to God he refused to side with his wife and called her foolish (Job 2:9-10) That gesture pleased God, but Adam sided with Eve instead of giving her a rebuke. But Job remained loyal to God, and God restored his life and destiny because of loyalty.

People said all sort of things against Job but he never lost his focus on God, he still honored God and was still loyal to Him regardless. Chaos is there to test your loyalty towards God and whom you serve. Judas was disloyal to Jesus Christ; he only cared about Jesus Christ when he was in charge of the money (John 12:4-8), in other words, he only hanged with Jesus Christ because he was having his way, loyalty is having your way or not, but believing it will be better. He that promised will make it good.

God heard Moses' sister complaining about Moses marrying a black woman, and God came out in the pillar of the cloud. God had to stand in the gap for Moses against his folks; you don't have to prove anything. God was mad when people said things against his servant, when God dealt with Mariam, she became a leper. Because of that everyone started to honor Moses, there were no more complaint, but everyone started to call Moses "Alas my Lord" (Numbers 12:2-15). Why because when you mess with who is loyal to God, God will show up on that person behalf and deal with you. Some people have died unnecessary because of messing around with someone who is loyal to God.

King Saul was disloyal to God but loyal to men, when confronted by the Prophet Samuel he said I feared the people, and obeyed their voice (2 Samuel 15:24). The people said let's sacrifice and he listened to them, his pride did hurt him and he lied to the man of God (2 Samuel 15:22-26).

Today people do likewise in the Pulpit. "I have feared the people so I preached a soft message so they don't leave." or "I have preached that message so the biggest giver in church does not get offended and leave." You need to preach what the Holy Spirit reveals to you. He kept what was forbidden and trying to please people than to be loyal (1 Samuel 15:9-24), but because he was disloyal, his throne was given to another. His leadership was given to King David (1 Samuel 15:28). The people who did great work in the Bible are people who were loyal to God.

Wherever you are assigned, be loyal because if you are disloyal your throne and your calling will be assigned to another, you will still have the gift but the role will be given to someone else. Reuben was disloyal; he slept with his father's concubine (Genesis 35:22) and his leadership was passed down to Joseph, he was still considered as the first born, but when it came to leadership Joseph was the head. It does not mean because someone was disloyal to you, you will have to do likewise. The Word of God said when we are faithless God remains faithful (2 Timothy 2:13), God is still loyal to us when we are not loyal to him. Loyalty is a big deal with God, and he loves those who are loyal to him.

Many people are loyal to their friends and disloyal to God, you tell people all the problems you may have, you believe the words of your friends than what the bible said about you, you don't even run to God when you have bad news or good news, instead of running to the throne you run to the phone, and that action alone is an act of disloyalty, because when you are loyal and you face an issue your first and last resort shall be towards the person you Love and Honor and that person is Jesus Christ, you run to God alone and He will reward you for being loyal to Him.

My prayer every day is to honor and be loyal to the right people in life. I hope you become like that as well, pray to God to teach you how to be loyal to the right people in life.

CHAPTER FIFTY-FOUR
HONESTY IS THE BEST POLICY

⇄

"Better is the poor that walk in his integrity "Honesty" than he that is perverse in his lips, and is a fool." (Proverbs 19:1)

Honesty is the best policy; whosoever came up with this saying is right. You can only be helped to the level of your need. You know when someone checks into rehab they are asked what they need help for, the rehab center might have a clue of how to deal with the person, but it's always best to hear from the person involved so they can be assist properly. God can't help you if you are not honest with your request, He will forgive you but He won't help you unless you have determined to change and you really need His help. You have to be honest with yourself, you may fool everyone else, but later on the real truth will come out that you really need help, so why wait to get worse then seek help? Many people in the church are broken and not honest with themselves and with God. Many people have trusted their pastor, assistant pastor, deacon and so forth. Their business was put out on the street and they have been shut down, at the hospital when someone gets diagnosed with a sickness they keep it confidential, well when a sheep comes for help, don't put the sheep's business out there. One, it diminishes your integrity and character; and second, the person offended is hard to be won back (Proverbs 18:19), you have just handed that soul to satan, because the accusation and guilt kicks in and now everyone knows about it. And the offended person will stop coming to church because they feel violated of the privacy and the trust they had in you. Please don't take your sheep's honesty in vain, but be a good shepherd to your sheep.

See, satan is looking for opportunities like that to drive away the sheep, he is the *accuser of the brothers* (Revelation 12:10). I love the incident of the woman caught in act of adultery, I love the wisdom of Jesus Christ in this moment, He said, "Which one of you has no sin, cast your stone upon her," and they all left, they could see the other person's weakness but could not see their own until the light came on, they were convicted and left, and Jesus Christ said, "Your accusers are not here anymore, go and sin no more," (John 8:4-11). That is the heart of a shepherd, He didn't condemn her, He comforted her and told her don't do this again. But it was an act of love and grace and she was changed for impact.

CHAPTER FIFTY-FIVE
BE A HISTORY MAKER, NOT A STORY TELLER, LOOK AT THE STORY TELLER

⇄

"And they went and came to Moses, and to Aaron, and to all the congregation of the children of Israel, into the wilderness of Paran, to Kadesh; and brought back word into them, and into the congregation, and showed them the fruit of the land.

"And they told him, and said, we came into the land whither you sent us, and surely it flows with milk and honey; and this is the fruit of it.

"Nevertheless the people are strong that dwell in the land, and the cities are walled, and very great: and moreover we saw the children of Anak there.

"The Amalekites dwell in the land of the south: and the Hittites, and the Jebusites, and the Amorites, dwell in the mountain: and the Canaanites dwell by the sea, and the coast of Jordan." (Numbers 13:26-29)

Look at the history maker

"And Caleb stilled the people before Moses, and said, let us go up at once, and possess it; for we are well able to overcome it." (Numbers 13:30).

Look at the story teller

"But the men that went up with him said, we are not able to go up against the people; for they are stronger than we.

"And they brought up an evil report of the land which they had searched into the children of Israel, saying the land, through which we have gone to search it, is a land that eat up the inhabitants thereof; and all the people that we saw in it are men of a great stature.

"And there we saw the giants, the sons of Anak, which come of the giants: and we were in our own sight as grasshoppers, and so we were in their sight" (Numbers 13:31-33)

Be a history maker and not a story teller. David made history with Goliath, Joshua and Caleb made history by taking over the promise land. You can do it as well, the same God that helped them, is with you—He is the same yesterday today and forever (Hebrews 13:8).
In order to believe all of these we got to study God's word and believe it.

Look what many people have been taught, in order to grow you have to go to church, that is not true, the church is not the building, you are the church and if you don't grow how will the church grow, the building may grow in numbers but not in discipleship. I would rather have two people who are dedicated and making an impact than having 1000 that just fill the building and not willing to grow.

Today we see the impact of the gospel because it was done by people who were willing and longing to grow. Your pastor is 30% responsible for your spiritual growth, but you are 70% responsible for your growth. Your pastor will not read books for you, he will not fast for you all the time. You come to church 2 times a week; what do you do the remaining 5 days; is up to you to manage.

At some point you have to take over and be responsible over your destiny and display the goodness of God in you, "Christ in you the hope of glory," (Colossians 1:27). You have to do your own Bible reading and study; because everyone has to answer for himself before God (Romans 14:12).

You are born to make history and not to tell stories. Sometimes people are afraid to rebuke those who aren't preaching or teaching the truth. Jesus Christ rebuked his disciples and elders in the church when they tried to run the house of God based on tradition and information but not revelation. The Bible said the tradition of men has made the Word of God of none effect (Romans 3:3). God hates tradition because tradition corrupts the people not to enter into their God called greatness.

God is not amused by a tradition; He is interested in His Word that is born out of the revelation given by the Holy Spirit. If people continue in tradition it will continue to be recycled. You were created for impact and not to be lukewarm. Christ is in us, why should we be afraid? The Bible says, "If God be for us who can be against us." (Romans 8:31). I wonder where are the Elijah's of our days? By God's grace you are the Elijah of today, tomorrow and until Christ comes. Stand for what is right and stand for God.

When Jesus Christ was going to the cross He rebuked Peter for trying to make excuses for Him not to go on the cross, so Peter wanted to prove Jesus Christ that he was with Him by cutting the soldier's ear (John 18:10-11). Jesus Christ rebuked him because He didn't want Peter to stop the will of God over His life, Jesus Christ loved Peter but He refuses to let Peter mess up what Heaven has scheduled for our salvation.

There should be no competition in the Kingdom, all we want is fruit. Jesus Christ said I'm here to do the will of the Father. While it is day, I work. Work while you are alive because when you are dead you can't work for God anymore. That's what Jesus was telling us, work when God has given you days here on earth. But when you die, there is no return to finish what you should have done.

Jesus cursed the fig tree, (Mark 11:20) that fig tree was under demonic delay, He had to curse it because He didn't want that curse of delay to dominate that city, for who the Son sets free is free indeed. It is the will of God for everyone to be saved and come to the knowledge of God, we have to pray and reach out to those nobody wants to reach; and go places, where no one dares to go. One of the disciples asked Jesus, "How will the world know you?" (John 14:22-23) They will know Him by the power of evangelism and the demonstration of the gospel, also through the impartation to display the Kingdom The woman at the well received a Word and was transformed. She went on to impact others and her life changed and wanted everybody else to witness what she witnessed. She started to evangelize for the kingdom. Jesus Christ did not come to teach or preach Jesus, but He came to introduce us to the kingdom.

One thing I know for sure, he that stays under the rain gets wet, and he that touches fire gets burned, and he that touches the power of God will never remain the same. When you hook up with God, you make history, because God will take you places where only the hand of God can take you. Stop telling stories, but take on challenges that make history.

CHAPTER FIFTY-SIX
RESTRUCTURE

⇌

"Behold, the hire of the labourers who have reaped down your fields, which is of you kept back by fraud, crieth: and the cries of them which have reaped are entered into the ears of the Lord of Sabbath." (James 5:4)

Many of the problems we see in the world are not random problems, they are structure problems. The structure problem started in the church and now God is in the position to fix it. Some people in leadership were placed in those positions by spiritual fraud; satan placed them in those positions for his benefit. But God will expose many problems to them that they cannot solve in order to dethrone them from those positions, and place the right people in their positions. Many thought they were called to open churches and pastor a church because they wanted honor. Many were suppose to be armor bearers, but because of pride and praises of people went on to become pastors and occupy the place where others ought to be. God is going to expose them to problems beyond their anointing, if they were called by God, they will be able to solve those problems without sweat, but if they weren't called for those positions, they will be demoted.

God is in the process of restructuring the church and the world. Only those who are in the right position will have the answers to any problems that come their way and the positions they occupied. People thought that this was a depression or a recession, it's not a depression or a recession, but the Kingdom restructure. The Bible says in Proverbs 29:2 that when the righteous are in authority, the people rejoice: but when the wicked bear rule, the people mourn.

People have mourned enough because of the wicked in authority, gas is too high because money has to be saved for election or lavish lifestyles, mortgage is high because someone wants to be rich fast, time is coming when houses are easy to afford, and gas will be as cheap as you want it. Some heads of state shouldn't be in the positions they are, some senators shouldn't be anymore, some leaders shouldn't be in leadership anymore, many don't qualify in the positions they occupy. There are no shortages in the world, the only shortage we are witnessing is because the wrong people are placed in positions they were not called for, once the right people are in place, God will open their eyes for abundance, God has to close the eyes of many people in many positions because if their eyes are open; they will amass wealth and afflict the righteous with evil, perversion, idolatry, and so forth. Now is the time to seek God and be faithful in order to be positioned, because it will happen fast, that's why the Bible says, "Many that are first shall be last; and the last first" (Mark 10:31). Those who were first are there because they were cheaters under satanic radar, now God is avenging "the righteous" that are last while they are supposed to be first.

Stop looking all over the place for answers—seek God because it's not a depression it's the kingdom restructure. Satan has used false and corrupted leaders to change the laws for his advantage, now God will be placing people in those positions to reverse the laws. The righteous in authority are coming in place. Don't be surprised if such a pastor is no longer pastoring, but a counselor at the church—it's the Kingdom restructure. Some will try to resist this plan of God, sickness will hit them and rejection will set in unless they surrender.

If you see your old boss driving the bus, don't pity him or her, it's the Kingdom restructure. If you see the lady that was giving you a hard time at work before, and now she is a sales person in a store, and walking your goods into your luxury car, don't feel bad, it's the kingdom restructure. If you see that man who thought he was "all that" at the company you worked for before, but now he is picking up your garbage in front of your mansion, don't be surprised—it's the Kingdom restructure. It's not the depression but it's the Kingdom restructure.

CHAPTER FIFTY-SEVEN
WE HAVE FAILED BIG MAMA

⇄

What is happening to the new generation? So many people have lost their self-identity. Grandmas want to be called aunty and refuse to be called grandma. There is a crack in the foundation in today's way of living. Back in the day, our grandparents were present and made sure they put in us the values that represent them. They have sacrificed, they have prayed, and we still see the evidence of their prayers in many people today. They have achieved the impossible against all odds, they did not have technology but they had God, values, and common sense. They sacrificed for the generation to come. Now the way things are going today, I'm wondering where all the grandma's are. It seems like we have failed the grandmas who gave their all for us. They fought for human rights, they fought for the right to vote, they fought so one day black and whites will sit together ride on the same bus; they did not have the privilege to read, but they had the wisdom of someone who have been awarded a master in divinity.

I'm asking the question; where did we drop the ball? It used to be everybody in the community would raise the child that was out of course, and made sure that child makes it in life. Where are those grandmas who cared so much about the future of a nation by teaching those around them values, respect, the fear of God, and the love of Jesus Christ to those who receive Him and heard them. Where are the grandmas that dropped everything when a child had challenges in life and nurture them to be better? Today many grandmas are after boyfriends and have rejected the sacrifice there grandmas did for them. I cry to God to challenge our hearts, that we awake to righteousness and be there for each other and raise a generation of successful, God fearing men and women.

One generation should advance the next generation and they have done that, but we haven't done so for the next generation so far. Right now we have an epidemic of children raising children—this has to be reversed. They carry the title *mother* or *father* but don't act like it. We have failed big mamas who have sacrificed for us and taught us well. Now we have become so greedy that the generation before us does not have more than we do now, but with the little they had they made it last, they had value and love few of us carry today. They were loyal and carrying. Today, people are driven by money and greed. Nobody is willing to sacrifice for the next generation, everyone wants to be famous and forsake what is right for what they think is more important. Women hear me—examine yourselves; and let's make sure we do not fail the last generation. Let's make Big Mama proud by remembering them and exercising what they have taught us. Respect, love, honor, and the fear of God.

CHAPTER FIFTY-EIGHT
EVIL LABORATORY

⇄

The devil has an evil laboratory, the homosexual and lesbian, they were not born that way, their genes and sexual orientation were switched at an evil laboratory. God will not give you a wrong gender, that's why He is God, because He can't make mistakes. He is all knowing and all sufficient. If God makes a mistake, the whole world is over—the stars will be falling, the sea will rise and the world will be flooded. God can't make mistakes, He is the only person who can't afford a mistake at any time. We can make mistakes, but He can't. Those who can see in the spiritual realm understand this; God is not into perversion but into holiness. That's why it is important to pray and read books that edify the spirit man. Anything done by satan can be reversed by the Word of God. That's why, when you see your child acting abnormal, do not take it lightly. Make it a prayer subject, pray it now so you don't have to pray it anymore.

Even some people have fallen sick and the sickness was produced in the evil laboratory. Why would God heal someone with aids if it was from God? Why would God heal you from cancer if it was from him? Many sicknesses people suffer today are engineered in evil laboratories. That is one of the venues witches and wizard uses to afflict people—thru evil laboratories. With no argument at all—some of the sickness people face, are the result of our own faults and sins. Yet many of them are the work of an evil laboratory. I pray that you come to the knowledge of God and grow in prayer and repentance. A woman with a woman and a man with a man, what sort of confusion is that. God is not the author of confusion but of sound mind (1 Corinthians 14:33). "For God has not given us the spirit of fear; but of power, and of love, and of a sound mind," (2 Timothy 1:7).

I hope people realize that God is not the one to be mad at—instead, be mad at the devil. It is evil if your child has an issue with their sexual orientation, don't give up. Make it a fasting and prayer issue, bring it before God, and let God reverse that plague that has come in your house. He promised you that no plague shall come near your dwelling (Psalm 91:10). Let God arise and perfect what concerns you (Psalms 138:8).

Don't give up, God can still restore your children's health and life. When people go to the hospital, especially those who are expecting; they go for the ultra sound and they are told on the spot if the baby she is carrying will not come out right, and that is the work of an evil laboratory. In that moment, all the world of darkness needs is your agreement that the child will be that way.

Very often in those situations you are offered to have an abortion and when you agree to do it, that blood is used in an evil laboratory to balance evil accounts. That's why it is good to be mature and grow in the Word of God so when you face situations like that, you can rebuke it. I know many people who were told that their child will be deformed at birth, but because they took it in prayer and rebuked that evil report that came from the evil laboratory, the child came out without being deformed. Why would God give you a child that will cause you pain, a child is supposed to bring joy. Don't be concerned, God said He will perfect that which concerns you. When you are expecting, shield that pregnancy in the blood of Jesus Christ.

Remember Jacob? He received a vision that he was able to use a certain strategy in order to come up with a certain kind of breed of livestock. The skin design of that livestock was never seen in the world, it was an idea produced and given by Heaven's laboratory (Genesis 30:30-43). I remember the day I was inspired to write about Heaven's restructure. In that evening, I had a vision: I saw a young man walking and I saw that a man slapped him and he fail, and someone rushed to call his parents. They picked him up and tried to rush him to the hospital. The young man couldn't talk anymore and was not aware what was going on because he was in a coma. I came towards them and I asked them if I can pray for the young man and they said "yes." So I prayed for him and he was still not okay. They went on to the hospital and I asked the Holy Spirit why he could not get healed and He said He wanted to show me something.

So I was quiet and was watching (still at sleep as a person but my spirit was awake). They got to the hospital and the suggestion was to put the boy under medication because they diagnosed him with a rare sickness. I asked the Holy Spirit what was that for, and He said the young man's sickness was evil because of his calling, the goal is to get him sick so he can't fulfill his destiny. He said my prayer did work because God used that to heal the young man, and He said that's why there is a recession and depression; because God wants to place people in the right field. There are doctors called by God; when they see a patient, the Spirit of God will reveal to them if that sickness is evil driven or a natural cause, and they will pray for that person and the person will be whole in the moment because they will carry the anointing of healing upon them. I saw the young man rise up and walk—then I woke up.

That was eye opening. After the dream I received an attack in my sleep, a group of gangs attacked me and they were asking me why I prayed for the young man that it was none of my business. They wanted to jump on me—then I woke up and started to pray against any satanic gang attacks. I forbid their agenda to violate my life, the life of my wife and children, or any of my family members in any way, shape, or form in the name of Jesus Christ. I saw it in the spirit—if I do nothing about it, it will manifest in the natural. So I did. Your spirit is very powerful, I knew it was powerful but when I saw that encounter with the young man in the spirit and how I fought that group; I was surprised to see how much power your spirit has.

There is a man who used to be a satanist and he was giving his testimony. He said that he went for his training in the cemetery, because the cemetery is where satan trains many of his people at night. He said that one night while in training, as they went into the cemetery; a tomb opened up and he saw the stairs and they went down, the demon that was training him gave him something small that looked like popcorn as he started to chew. That thing started to enlarge in his mouth and his mouth became foamy he was then given water to drink. He said that exercise had reversed his eye sight, he could see insect intestines and he could see a baby in a stomach before the woman knows she is pregnant. If he can, he would cause either miscarriage or afflict the baby in the womb even dedicating the child to the world of darkness.

See, he was in the cemetery under a tomb inside an evil laboratory planning evil. These are secrets that satan has many Christians not knowing about. I have heard a testimony of a great man of God Bishop David Oyedepo, he was on the mission field doing God's work and he came home and saw his wife crying. He asked her what was wrong and she said she was having a miscarriage and he could see the blood all over the place, the evidence was there, but I love the boldness he had. He said, "My child will not die but live," from the time he prayed to the time the baby was born was exactly 9 months, his child was born and he is alive and well. He had to do something and take authority over that evil report, he knew it wasn't of God, if he didn't do anything about it he would have lost that child and maybe the one after that. Because he did put a stop to it, the devil wouldn't dare trying again. Abortion and miscarriage is not of God, it is an evil sacrifice. Babies dying after birth is not of God, its evil. Your baby coming out deformed is not of God. Whenever you plan to have a child seal that pregnancy very well in the blood of Jesus Christ.

When my wife was pregnant with my son Canaan, I was in prayer one day and God told me to seal her pregnancy with the blood of Jesus Christ, when I heard it I did it right away and when I prayed over the baby using anointing oil as a point of contact to seal it. I tell you she was only 4 weeks into her pregnancy, but as soon as I said, "I seal this pregnancy with the blood of Jesus Christ," the baby moved in her belly.

I understand that in this moment the baby is not big yet, but whatever was being done in the world of darkness had to realize that this pregnancy was under Heaven's covering, and that no one could use the blood of my child for an evil sacrifice, God has the purpose for my child and I'm not letting satan and an evil laboratory have reason over my child. I write you this by experience and I hope you take this to heart. That's why it is good to have a child while married, because satan can't accuse you before God, but I thank God for his grace that He gives us time to make it right with Him, even in our mistakes.

CHAPTER FIFTY-NINE

PSALM 23, SHEEP OF THE SHEPHERD

⇄

The Lord is my shepherd; I shall not want. This is a shepherd talking. King David realized that he is a shepherd to the sheep, but also he realized that he is a sheep to a Shepherd. This is what helped King David achieve great things in his lifetime. He realized that as a shepherd it was his duty to care for his sheep and make sure they are in safety and that the wolf come not to steal them. Notice that the pulpit is higher than the pews, why? It is a spiritual secret and law; it is like that so the shepherd can see what is going on in the spiritual realm and warn the sheep while he stands on guard. A shepherd provides, give assurance, protect and leads in the presence of God. A good shepherd does not split his sheep—he assembles them and protects them from the wolf.

A good shepherd gives the sheep what they need and they obey his voice. A good shepherd, prays for his sheep and shares the heart of God with them and leads them in the way of peace. Being anointed with oil does not means that you are anointed, many people were anointed with oil, but because their heart was not good, the anointing did not stay. The anointing stayed on King David because his heart was pure before God, Eliab could not have kept the anointing because his heart was not pure, he may have been good looking but that did not impress God to urge Prophet Samuel to anoint him (1 Samuel 16:6-7).

King David's heart of the shepherd pleased God and when he was anointed, the anointed stayed on him (1 Samuel 16:11-13); when you have the heart of the shepherd you please God. The church is not a center of saints, but of the broken as well. Time does not heal; the fact of following that broken, hurt souls; it will cause healing. Remember you are a shepherd to your sheep and you are a sheep to your Shepherd (which is Jesus Christ). You will answer to Him if you don't care for your sheep well.

Jesus Christ said, "What you have given me Father, I have lost none," (John 18:9). I'm sure He had meetings with His followers teaching them about Ministry and how to make the church grow and so forth. That would be a powerful session to be part of—round table with King Jesus Christ. I don't get Pastors that lose members and are okay with it. If you believe that member belongs to you, you got to be outraged when you lose them, outraged in the spirit. A shepherd lost one sheep and he went all over town looking for it until he found it (Matthew 18:12-14) that is the heart of the shepherd. The Bible says that Heaven rejoices when a soul repents (Luke 15:7). Remember, you are a shepherd and as a shepherd you are a sheep to a Shepherd, Jesus Christ. You will have to answer to Him for everything you do.

Pride has caused a lot of pastors let satan have their sheep by giving cold responses such as: I'm not calling them, I'm not doing this. You are the shepherd and your heart must ache when the sheep is lost and you know they should be part of your flock. If they are not part of your flock then it is okay, at least pray for them that God leads them to the right shepherd.

Peter betrayed Jesus Christ, Jesus Christ did everything for him yet he denied Him when he was dealing with his purpose. But Jesus Christ when He was resurrected made sure that He did not lose his flock. He assembled the disciples in one room including Peter and still used him for the gospel. That is the heart of the shepherd. He came back for Thomas making sure he witness the power and Love of God even in doubt so the world do not steal him and cast him into hell, Jesus Christ showed him His hands and proved to him that God is real and that Jesus Christ is the real Shepherd, I imagine how Thomas felt after Jesus Christ showed up in the room, many told him they saw the Lord, and he has missed quite few opportunities to see Him for himself. Jesus Christ showed up just for Thomas (John 20:24-28), that is the ministry heart of the shepherd.

Time and guilt of betray did not heal Peter. It was the compassion that Jesus Christ showed him that healed Peter and perfected his ministry. The compassion of Jesus Christ made a difference in his life (Jude 1:22) and He helped them from not failing and He presented them faultless before God (Jude 1:24). The way you treat your sheep shows how much you value them. No shepherd will mistreat his sheep when he knows how valuable the sheep are.

CHAPTER SIXTY
VALUE THE GIFT AROUND YOU

⇄

Many Christians are like surfers looking for another wave to ride on, and when the wave does not come, they get disappointed. A lot of believers are driven by performance. The Kingdom of God doesn't function by performance, it functions by Heaven's agenda. God does not speak every day, he could if he wants to. The man at the pool of Bethesda could have been healed sooner than expected, but the Bible said an angel came in a certain season into the pool, and troubled the water: whosoever then went first after the troubling of the water stepped in was made whole of whatsoever disease he had (John 5:3-4). If you are not engaged in what God is saying where you are planted and someone who came in few days and get engaged in the teaching of the man of God that person will get blessed.

Your man of God can only flow based on the demand you place on God. His anointing will only respond to your need. God will only pour water on ground that is thirsty; God does not cast his pearls before swine (Matthew 7:6). The best word God reserves for those who value His Word and His servant. God reserve his deepest revelation for Eagles and not for Swine. Many members disqualify obeying their Pastor when he does not do miracles like before, or when he stops prophesying like before, in everything there is a season.

If you are under a Pastor who prophesies every day and lays hands on you every time; you got to wonder. There is a season of prophesy, then can come a season of prayer to carry on the prophesy, then can come a season of deliverance to cleanse your spiritual bloodline and pipe in order to function in the capacity God wants you to function then it could be a season of silence just teaching and exhortation and healing, all those could be the gift your Pastor, Prophet, Evangelist may carry, so you will have to shift when the Spirit of God makes the shift. Many people in the church are more in love with the spectacle than hearing what the spirit of God is saying in the moment. The church has to grow up and be like the children of Issachar who understood the times, and told Israel what to do (1 Chronicles 12:32).

Few believers honor the gift that is given to them. Many don't at all because of familiarity—Jesus Christ could not do miracle in a certain place because people knew him since he was a child and the Bible said, "He could not do mighty works there because of unbelief," unbelief did not start over night it's because they did not honor the gift that was around them and God had to move him elsewhere, where His gift will be honored (Matthew 13:55-58). If you don't value your man of God, who else will value him? If you don't value your man of God you are the one missing out, the Word you could need at that moment is in his mouth. Peter had an issue, he did need to pay his taxes and Jesus Christ told him the first fish you catch take the gold out of his mouth and pay the taxes, see the word that is in the mouth of your man of God is gold (Matthew 17:24-27). If your Pastor has more to say when is out there to another church than when he is in his own, it shows that God is not allowing his spirit on the man of God be wasted because whatever he may do it will be fruitless because there is no honor of his gift in the room, God rather use him where his gift is most needed and valued. See, Samson spent time with Delilah because she made him comfortable but he found comfort in the wrong place with a woman who could be corrupted easily, while the enemies were busy planing to kill Samson what was Israel doing to preserve him? He was called, he had flaws, but that did not make his call to be taken away from him by God, he was still called. The Philistines were busy trying to kill Samson but what was Israel doing to preserve Samson to live a long life?

They have said you have fallen but they never took time to fast and pray for you while your enemies were busy planning a plot against your man of God (Judges 16:4-21), they thought they got Samson and that he was finished, but they forgot that even though they found the strength in his hair, but they forgot that he still has the gene that makes the hair grow and his hair grew and the strength came back and he was able to kill and destroy (Judges 16:22-31). People may laugh at their pastor because he failed, but as long he still knows God, God can restore him. Watch out, if he repents and lines back up with God, he will still do wonders. Even in failure, still honor the gift that is around you, because God can still restore. I pray that you open up and honor the gift that you have in your pulpit and pews and watch God do wonders in your midst.

CHAPTER SIXTY-ONE
PRAYING IN TONGUES

⇄

Praying in tongues is one of the secret weapons for believer. The Bible says, "Let's not be ignorant of satan devices lest [he] take advantage of you," (2 Corinthians 2:11). See, the only advantage satan has over the believer is ignorance. Satan's only strength is the ignorance of the saints. Whatever you do in life, please avoid being ignorant. Knowledge is power. The Apostle Paul said, "...I pray in tongues more than all of you," (1 Corinthians 14:18).

That should tell you something. I believe the reason he walked in such revelation and wrote most of the new testament is because of his praying in tongues. The Bible says that when you pray in tongues you speak not to men but to God and you speak mysteries (1 Corinthians 14:2). Wow! So when you pray in tongues satan is confused; he can't understand that language. You can pray in your native language, but there comes a dimension in prayer that in order to receive certain answers and revelation, you have to shift in a different language and that language connects you to the supernatural and that language is praying in tongues. The Holy Spirit will give you interpretation of what you just prayed about when you ask for it.

There is a study done by the health department saying 95% of all rare diseases do not have a single FDA (Food and Drug Administration) approved drug treatment. There are currently 400 treatments approved by the FDA for the nearly 7,000 rare diseases which have been identified. According to the estimate from NIH (National Institutes of Health), it will take 10,000 years at the current rate of the FDA drug approval to find therapies for all people suffering from rare and genetic diseases. In order to get revelation and to get quick result, is by praying in tongues. I believe no one will live 10,000 years and I believe the healing is needed right now.

Jesus Christ said that He must go in order for us to be like Him, and what made the ministry of Jesus Christ complete, was the ministry of the Holy Spirit. He had to get baptized by John in order to activate the Holy Spirit (John 1:32). Look what He did in three years of ministry. Still now we see the impact of His work, why? Because what He did was born of the spirit and not of the flesh, so when you pray in tongues you pray in the spirit and you are praying the perfect will of God (Romans 8:26-27). The Bible also says that when you pray in tongues you, "Build yourself up in your most Holy faith," (Jude 1:20). I have heard and visited certain churches where they do not believe in speaking in tongues, I wondered if they don't know the benefit of it or they just don't want to.

Apostle Paul said in 1 Corinthians 14:37-38, "If any man think himself to be a prophet, or spiritual, let him acknowledge that the things that I write unto you are the commandments of the Lord," also He said "but if any man be ignorant, let him be ignorant," I think we have to examine the Word of God here.

Jesus Christ said to his disciples to wait for the Holy Spirit in the book of Acts and when the Holy Spirit descended upon them they started to speak in unknown tongues and miracles took place (Acts 2:1-17). This was to fulfill God's Word where it says in Acts 1:16: men and women, this scripture must needs have been fulfilled, which the Holy Spirit by the mouth of King David spoke before concerning Judas, which was guide to them that took Jesus. It says "You shall receive power, after that the Holy Spirit is come upon you: and you shall be witnesses into me both in Jerusalem, and in all Judea, and in Samaria, and into the uttermost part of the earth." (Acts 1:8), if it's not God's will to speak in tongues why would Jesus tell his disciples to wait for the promise to receive the Holy Spirit? (Acts 1:4-5) That would have been a sign of disobedience on Jesus Christ part. Remember He said He does only what the Father tells Him to do, so if He told the disciples of the coming of the Holy Spirit that means the Father is okay that we receive the baptism of the Holy Spirit with evidence of speaking in tongues.

Jesus Christ said in John 7:38-40,

"He that believes on me, as the scripture has said, out of his belly shall flow rivers of living water. But this spake he of the

Spirit, which they that believe on him should receive: for the Holy Spirit was not yet given; because that Jesus Christ was not yet glorified. Many of the people therefore, when they heard this saying, said, of a truth this is the prophet."

Let me ask you a question, is Jesus Christ glorified? If your answer is yes then you can receive the baptism of the Holy Spirit with evidence of speaking in tongues. I heard a woman of God say one time that she went to minister in a certain country and in that city crime was insane—just chaos. When they started to pray in tongues in the midst of the gathering of the saints someone got a personal interpretation in their native tongue while they were praying in tongues and she was told where the person they were looking for was kept captive, the address, the location and who to talk to and they were able to retrieve their love one. I feel grieved for those who don't want to receive the baptism of the Holy Spirit with evidence of speaking in tongues.

See, Jesus Christ told the disciples to wait for this power, this should tell you something. I don't know why you can't take advantage of the privilege that is freely given to you. What I have written in this book it's the revelation given to me by praying in tongues and by doing personal bible study and the Holy Spirit open my eyes and my spirit to see what God wanted me to see, I pray that you get to experience that. This experience isn't for pastor, prophet, deacon only but it is for whosoever God will pour water upon whosoever is thirsty (Isaiah 44:3) my question to you is, are you thirsty to receive every promise and benefit God has available for you and praying in tongues is included in the package.

CHAPTER SIXTY-TWO
STAY HUMBLE

⇄

God resists the proud and He exalts the humble. God loves people who are humble, pride comes from the devil and not from God. In Isaiah 14:12-18 you see the devil exalting himself, saying that he is better than God and so forth. When Jesus Christ called His disciples, none of them had experience in ministry, but God called them and used them. Many people can talk and preach; the difference between the disciples and Jesus Christ was the character, not the calling. You can be called and do miracles and do mighty things, but your character can drown your purpose in life if it is stinky. Jesus Christ told Nicodemus, "You are a Rabbi in the church and you don't know what being born again means!" He was not mean about it, all He was telling him the cycle of wrong teaching and tradition needs to be broken and this the way you can tap into God without being bound by the law.

If you are a new pastor, prophet, or whoever you may be; it does matter what you are doing. Maybe God is using you to do miracles and people are praising you, be humble and have respect for elders, those who are in ministry before you, they can teach you things that will help you last in ministry. Being in ministry is not a joke and when you see someone who has been in ministry for a longtime you have to give them respect, many people don't make it and fall off along the way. Judas could not handle ministry, and he died an untimely death, God could have used anyone to betray Jesus Christ, but Judas' love of money and disloyalty caused him to sell out his soul to the devil.

Jesus Christ was so humble when the soldiers came to take Him away, they could not tell who He was because of His humility. The only way they could tell who He was, was when He spoke. He told them who are you seeking, they said Jesus Christ of Nazareth. And He said, "I am He whom you seek," and still they could not believe Him at His saying they thought it was a disguise but it wasn't (John 18:2-11) that is humility. Whatever you are doing, stay humble, it's not by your own strength, it's by the grace of God. The Bible said to compare not yourself one to another—it's not wise. It takes wisdom not to fall prey to the devil, when you start competing with your elders and others in The Lord you are set for failure because you are not operating in the spirit of humility and submission. 1 Peter 5:5-8 says, "Submit yourself to the elder, and be clothed with humility: for God resist the proud and give grace to the humble."

When you stay humble, the Bible says God will exalt you in due time. So there is time for everything, even when persecuted—cast your care upon Him because He cares for you. Many times people license the devil to strike on their lives. Since they did not stay humble the devil is ready to devour them. Devour means people running away from you, nobody can stand you anymore because you are too proud and so forth. That's how the devil devours these days, tarnishing your image and so forth. There is no competition instead let's work together as unto The Lord. Did Jesus Christ compete with the elders in the Synagogue? Not so, He did His part and went on to take care of God's business elsewhere.

The more humble you are, the more God promotes you. Whosoever criticizes you in ministry, don't mind them. They did not call you, God did. Stay focused on the One who called you to do the work (unless you have called yourself.) "Look up from whence come your help." (Psalms 121:1) God is your help. God will take care of those who are against you on your behalf, your job is to stay humble and focus. Remember this kind of battle is not yours but The Lord, God will plead your cause and will fight against them that fight against you (Psalms 35:1).

King David refused to touch King Saul, even when King Saul threw the javelin at him trying to kill him. The Bible said King David behaved himself wisely in all his ways; and the Lord was with him (1 Samuel 18:11-15). Because of his pride and his hurt, King Saul tried to kill King David many times, he wanted to kill him with the javelin even though he knew that God was with King David. He looked for King David everywhere trying to kill him but God did not deliver him into the hand of King Saul (1 Samuel 23:14) King Saul did not care at the moment but to do evil against the new comer "King" in Israel (1 Samuel 19:9-10). King David had the opportunity to kill King Saul, his entourage encouraged him to kill King Saul but he refused to listen to the counsel of the ungodly (Psalms 1:1-4) and remained humble; I like the response King Saul gave to King David when he found out that King David could have killed him when he had the opportunity to do so but decided to keep his integrity, and King Saul said to King David you are more righteous than I: for you have rewarded me good when I have rewarded you evil (1 Samuel 24:4-17) He had respect for the elders and his trust was in God. Saul tried to overthrow King David many times, but he couldn't because King David respected King Saul and God was on the look at out for King David.

Saul came to realize that his character was not good towards King David. King Saul's character got him in trouble, he was anointed, but God could not stand his character. He would rather please and fear people than God. He died in pride and refused to repent of his stinky character. He refused to seek God's help and crying out to God for mercy, but he would rather go see the fortune teller for his answers for the trouble he did put himself in (1 Samuel 28:6-18). Let God be your only option, not the world and satan's failing system. Even in times of chaos learn to be still and trust God (Psalms 46:10).

God will contend with those who contend with you (Isaiah 49:25). Because if you walk in offense you will lose defense, God is your defense, but offense can leave you hanging. Saul sought to kill King David. Everybody knew it and the women did not help the situation by singing a song they wrote while in the presence of

King Saul saying "King Saul killed his thousands and King David his ten thousands," beware of siding with those who want to kill you by encouraging you to be a rebel towards your elders. How do the mighty fall? King David said (2 Samuel 1:27) lack of character will cause you to fall.

Paul said, "Follow me as I follow Jesus Christ" (1 Corinthians 11:1), follow those who are leading you to God and not those who are leading you to satan. Those who are leading you to Jesus Christ are the people you need to follow. But those who are leading you away from Jesus Christ those are the people you need to run and stay away from, because evil company and communication corrupt good manners (1 Corinthians 15:33).

When you hang with good people, you get good manners, and when you hang with bad people you get bad manners, the law of association. You become what you associate with.

God will let you choose whatever you want. God gave Israel a King and they did not want it, then God gave them a King of their choice and still they were not happy about the choice.

Wait on God and you will not be disappointed at all. He knows what is best for you, the worse thing you could do is taking matters into your own hands and not believe God at his promise or his Word, He is the only one who can do the impossible for you. Regardless of the delay, still believe Him, He will surely bring it to pass. Abraham was promised a child—he had to wait years before that word and promise come to pass, but the Bible says he did not give up, but still believed God and it pleased God and he called him his friend (James 2:23). Humility brings patience and assurance, Abraham had to stay humble before God in order to have such patience to believe and honor God while he was waiting for his promise. Choose today regardless the set backs, regardless the length you will have to endure, tell yourself this I will be humble and let God be God in every situation you may face.

CHAPTER SIXTY-THREE
JESUS CHRIST IS COMING

$$\rightleftarrows$$

"But of that day and that hour know no man, no, not the angels which are in heaven, neither the Son, but the Father. Take you heed, watch and pray: for you know not when the time is.

"For the Son of man is as a man taking a far journey, who left his house, and gave authority to his servants, and to every man his work, and commanded the porter to watch.

"Watch you therefore: for you know not when the master of the house come, at even, or at midnight, or at cockcrowing, or in the morning:

"Lest coming suddenly he find you sleeping. And what I say unto you I say unto all, watch." (Mark 13:32-37).

The church has made a decision when Jesus Christ will come back, it shows how people teach and manage the gospel, that Jesus Christ will not come back under a broke, disorganized church all that sound good, it make sense. But the scripture tells us that Jesus Christ can come back at any time. When a thief comes to steal does he tell you when he is coming? Not at all, unless you get a hint somewhere and you prepare for it. The Word says in 1 Thessalonians 5:2, "...You know that the day of the Lord so comes as a thief in the night." Does that make Jesus a thief? No; it just warns us that as the thief comes without warning, so does the Son of God. The church has not been preparing for the coming of the Son of God, because if it did, the approach of spreading the gospel would have been at a very fast pace. The church is behind schedule and we need to move fast. Verse 32 of Mark 13 says that even the angels in heaven do not know when Jesus Christ is coming back "...Neither Jesus Christ himself, but the Father [God] only." The angels have been preparing for his coming a long time, nothing will catch them by surprise, even Jesus Christ has been preparing for the day of His coming, the question is will He find the church awake or at sleep when He comes back (Mark 13:36)? Based on everyones calling, Jesus Christ has left you in authority to do the work, also to watch for His coming (Mark 13:34). We have to be watchful for we don't know when He is coming back (Mark 13:35).

People may think they have time to repent, please don't jeopardize every opportunity you get to do God's work, to save, to teach, to pray, to repent and to be in order. This is a personal and collective work, that's why salvation is personal, also the Word of God said work your salvation with trembling, that's why Jesus Christ said that many will say to Him in that day, "I have done this or that in your name," and Jesus Christ's response will be, "I never knew you" (Matthew 7:22). Those who are saying "I did this in your name," are not lying, they are telling the truth. But if the time He comes you are not in order, yes, He does not know you—because you were not in order to be recognized as His, then you will be known as the devil's child because the blood was not applied before His coming for protection.

That's why we have to be ready always, stay humble, be at peace with everyone, stay away from pride, striving, and so forth; no one knows when He is coming. For those who do not believe this I pray that your eyes be open so you catch up with the plans of God and have the mind of Heaven, the Word says that even the devil believes there is a God (James 2:19), if the devil knows that, then He knows Jesus Christ is coming back. Be faithful wherever you are planted, for the Lord Jesus Christ is coming without warming. Church of Jesus Christ, rise and be on the move for His coming. This was one of the hardest chapters I had to write in this book, it is supposed to be the most delightful chapter to write, but it wasn't at the moment because it was eye opening to myself when the Holy Spirit was leading me to write it. Everyone will have the opportunity to hear the gospel in their lifetime before the coming of Jesus Christ (Titus 2:11-14), when you hear, do not hesitate to repent and get your life in order, because the Holy Spirit will give us a hint that a major moment is about to take place. But discernment is key in your relationship with the Trinity.

CHAPTER SIXTY-FOUR
BEWARE OF CORRUPTED LEADERS

$$\rightleftarrows$$

"Be not deceived: evil communications corrupt good manners"
(1 Corinthians 15:33)

Listen, be not deceived, when you deal with leaders, be aware of corrupt leaders. Don't side with them because of the spotlight you will gain, don't side with them because of donations and favor you may obtain for later on. Do not do these at all, when election time comes the house of God becomes a visiting ground to seek vote and to remain in office, but while you were in office for 3 years or more you never visited the house of God, you have never paid your tithe, you don't have a home church. If so, does your Pastor teach you the value of your position as a leader of the community or nation. I do not get this: they quote scriptures while on the pulpit when seeking the saint's vote, but when in office they are not willing to reject what is against the Word of God. They want the vote but don't want the correction of the Word of God.

The Word of God is meant to correct you into good works (2 Timothy 3:16-17) having a form of godliness, but denying the power thereof: from such turn away (2 Timothy 3:5). How can you be a leader and say you are with God and still sign a bill that allows homosexuals and lesbians to get married. You are okay with that, while the Word of God said, marriage is between a man and a woman, God said, "The man shall leave his Parents and cleave to his wife and they shall be one flesh," it's not a made up law it is scripture (Genesis 2:21-24; Mark 10:6-9). How can you be with God and allow the Bible to be taken out of schools? When you love God it shows through your actions. Also when you fear God, it shows through your words. All they say is not us, we don't want to offend anyone. The best thing is to listen to the people, what people are you listening to? Those who sponsor your elections and the heathens that can't stand the name of Jesus Christ, those are the ones who are called the people and not the saints.

The book of Colossians tells us to be aware of people who try to manipulate the Word of God for their own advantage and deceive many along the way because they just want their share. You don't need their donation. you are in Jesus Christ and you are complete in Him. (Colossians 2:6-10) That's what the Bible said in Colossians. Verse 8 says to beware lest any man spoil you through philosophy and vain deceit, after the tradition of men, and after the rudiments of the world, and not after Jesus Christ.

The church has to be bold in making its position known to those who are not for the Church of Jesus Christ, you know when they vote evil into law they don't need the church's consent, they do it without, but when it comes to vote the church is needed; we need to examine these deceptions and take a stand. When same sex is put in law, it does not affect the church only, but households and generations. If God destroyed Sodom and Gomorrah because of the sin of perversion that should ring a bell in your ear (Genesis 19:5). They wanted to rape the angels that came to see Lot and save him before God destroyed that city, what saved Lot, was that he was not living that lifestyle, also Lot was saved because of the prayer of his uncle Abraham.

God wants leaders that will follow His Word and consent with Him (Zephaniah 3:9). The church has to rise up and say no to what is not of God, and say yes to what advances the Kingdom of God. A godly leader will declare a fast and firmly speak up against any law that is against the Word and thoughts of God; we don't see it these days because the church has kept quiet and guilty of agreement made in secret, carnal and corrupted. We declare a fast in the churches but not in offices, we claim one nation under God and do not act like it, we proclaim God bless America but we have not blessed God by obeying His Word and fearing Him. The children of Israel were under the worse attack in their lives, genocide was declared against them, it took good leaders "Mordecai and Esther" to seek God's face by declaring a nationwide fast (Esther 4:15-17. Because of that, God changed their fate because they sought the face of God and stood on His promises for His people.

Our leaders must have the fear of God. Our leaders fear men more than they fear God, because they want the vote; they spend time in dinners to raise money for election but not any Word of God is mentioned in those meetings, but they dare going to church to seek votes. "If my people, which are called by my name, shall humble themselves, and pray, and seek my face, and turn from their wicked ways; I will hear from Heaven, and I will forgive their sin, and will heal their land." (2 Chronicles 7:14) the healing of the land is in repentance and not in fund raising. Church of Jesus Christ: stand your ground and regain your respect as a reigning church. Do you know 100 saints can decide an outcome of an election? Because the authority of the saints can shift the atmosphere.

CHAPTER SIXTY-FIVE
LEADERSHIP

⇄

"You shall know them by the fruit," (Matthew 7:16-28).

Leadership is not just a title; it's the fruit you leave behind. Everybody can claim to be a leader; but the proof is in the putting. Jesus Christ was a leader; we see the fruit he left behind, Dr. Martin Luther King was a leader, Nelson Mandela, Booker T Washington, George Washington Carver were leaders, look at the fruit and impact they have left behind. Moses, Joshua, David, all these were leaders that have made differences in their times until now we witness the result of their leadership.

"If the blind lead a blind, both shall fall into a ditch" (Luke 6:39), the ditch is a pit or a place of trouble and sorrow, if your leader is causing you sorrow, question his leadership, he may be blind in the direction he is leading you, no excuses, you want fruit—not just a title. You don't just need words, you need action and proof, the Bible said faith is the title deed proof (Hebrews 11:1 AMP) you need proof or vote him out of office. Don't play with people's destinies like that, you can't hold back people's lives like that. If you can't lead, stop and let someone else do the job. Many times the best service you can do to yourself is to admit you can't lead above your leadership knowledge; it is not a sign of weakness but a sign of strength. That is one of the problems in Africa and other countries where so called leaders who are blind and refuse to get out of the way. God had enough with Pharaoh, the cry of the people was so much God had to do something about it, because He hates leaders who take captive the destinies of people through oppression and affliction. Violence is for the coward and conversation is for the strong.

Any person can be good or bad, it depends at the level of tolerance you give him, you have to play a part in every freedom you want and command your demand. Don't just sit there. Value your life as much you value your destiny, every destiny failure is a part of your participation in the failure. Are you participating in success, or in failure. Success is given to everyone in life, but successful people take on challenges that the unsuccessful run away from. So to be successful, take on challenges; and if you want to be unsuccessful, run away from challenges. David became King because he took on the challenge to fight Goliath (1 Samuel 17:32), while the rest ran from the challenge (1 Samuel 17:24).

See Goliath's resume was impressive, when they talk about him, you can easily fear (1 Samuel 17:4-6), that's what happened to those who ran from him, ignorance is not an excuse, they forsook their God and made Goliath bigger than their God. It took a man of revelation to fight him, King David was well trained in secret for this occasion because training is better than learning the hard way at the day of the event (1 Samuel 17:20-58). Mr. Mohamed Ali said he hated every minute of training but he made up his mind by saying he rather suffer in training and live the rest of his life as a champion, decision is key in order to become great

Joshua and Caleb are well spoken of because they took on the challenge to possess the land, they should have had that land longtime ago, but because of fear of so called leaders who came with the evil report that's why it lasted this long. They could have died without possessing the land if nobody made the move to take on the challenge (Joshua 18:1-3). Joshua and Caleb stood on the promise of God (Joshua 23:5) and God gave them faith by reminding them what He did for them before (Joshua 24:8). When you focus on the Word of God so much and believe in it, it will start leading you and speaking to you (Proverbs 6:22). Even when it looked impossible to others in their sight to face the giants, but as long you got the Word of God, you become the giant and your enemy becomes the grasshopper. The nature of the grasshopper is to run whenever it feels the presence of something. See Joshua and Caleb is well spoken off all over the world but no one talks of the leaders who ran away from the challenge. Be a story maker and not a story teller

Many times God will keep you in the secret place and create a situation to promote you. King David spent his time in the secret place and God created an event to promote him as King of Israel, when he fought and overcame Goliath. You have to be bold and courageous in order to demand change. God told Abraham, "As far as you can see, I will give it to you, nobody can't lead you as far they don't see, even God can't bless you as far you can't see (Genesis 13:15). Because if you don't know the purpose of the thing you will start to worship the thing instead of Him, but when you understand the purpose, you worship God and use the thing for His glory.

If God did not see our salvation ahead, the sacrifice of Jesus Christ on the cross would have been a failure, the cross and resurrection was a success because God saw it before it took place in the natural, even the devil couldn't have seen it. He had the information that the Messiah will come, but he had no revelation not until King Jesus Christ was crowned in his place as the God above all god's. The Bible said if satan knew he would not have crucified the Lord of glory (1 Corinthians 2:8), who is the Lord of glory—it's Jesus Christ of Nazareth, King of Kings and Lord of Lord's. He is the Alpha and the Omega. The beginning and the end, He is all in all.

CHAPTER SIXTY-SIX
THE BOARD AND GOD

⇄

This topic is not new at all, it has been the issue in old days of the Bible. When the Pastor or leader comes up with a vision God has given him and the Pastor or leader bring it to the board, and the board challenges it for some reason—it could be lack of confidence, tradition, simply fear of losing their position in the church or on the board, or lack of knowledge, and so forth. When Jesus Christ came to raise Lazarus of Bethany (the brother of Mary and Martha) the priests and the pharisees were not happy that Jesus Christ was going to raise up Lazarus of Bethany, this is what they said, "For this Man does many Miracles, if we let Him alone, all men will believe on Him: and the Romans shall come and take away both our place and nation," they were so focused on their position and refused to embrace the change, because they are thinking only about losing their position because someone else is walking in greater revelation than they (John 11:47-48). This thing alone sometimes brings strife and jealousy even causing division to the point of braking the church, the pastor against the board, or the board against God.

This shouldn't be the time to argue when a vision is presented, because a house divided against itself can't stand (Matthew 12:25), and where there is strive there is confusion and evil work (James 3:16), this is the time to seek the face of God for confirmation, of What the Pastor has brought to the table, it's either the Pastor didn't hear God well or the board didn't hear God or did not seek the Lord. There shouldn't be a fight at all. Remember you are part of one body; you ought to work together and not fight each other, souls need to be saved. It's amazing how the board can shrink the vision God has for the church; and try to bring God to their level.

Anytime someone wants to shrink the vision it shows that the person is not grounded in the Word, but by tradition. It took two leaders that believed God to enter the promised land, while the 10 leaders caused people to cry and worry because of their unbelief. Their unbelief caused the people to think that God had lied to them (Numbers 14:1:3), based on what they have heard from the leaders, in their sight it was impossible to possess the land when God has promised it, but the two leaders knew it was possible because they believed God and had seen God do great things before (Numbers 13:27-33). See, many churches are governed by titles and not by the vision God has for the church. A church can't remain the same forever, you serve the God who is not conformed to monotony, He always has something new to bring, and we have to move along with Him, like the children of Israel, follow the cloud when it moves, don't stand still or you will miss out (Exodus 13:21-22).

You need to get in the boat and ride with the vision. Don't be Jonah in the camp, but be Peter in the boat and go for the challenge, or be Joshua and Caleb and believe the vision God has given your man of God, and support him for a house divided against self can't stand (Luke 11:17). Be the solid rock in bringing the vision to pass, it is God's vision not yours if God hasn't told you otherwise get in the boat and ride.

CLOSING WORD

In everything in life there are two ways, you can be poor, then become rich or you can be rich then become poor. You can be sick then be healed or you can be healthy then be sick. But there is only one thing that does not have a two way ticket and that is death. When you die it's either Heaven or hell. There is a African saying from the Congolese that says, if the catfish comes and tells you the crocodile is sick underwater believe him. Why? Because they live in the same environment. Jesus Christ told us hell and Heaven is real. You have to believe Him because He and the Father are one and live in the same environment. You know your life; think about it—if you die right now, where you think you will go? Remember, there is no in-between, it's either Heaven or hell. Every master has a master to report to, you will report to your Master, Jesus Christ of Nazareth regardless what position you possess. Regardless how much money, title, and friends you may have. God's Word will do what it should do and can't return void. Everybody was created by God to have a home church (a church that they attend faithfuly and belong to) and to be used by God to advance the Kingdom

Many people come to church mostly for four events, funerals, marriages, baby dedications, or graduations, if you can make the effort to come during those events, why not make it a priority to come to the house of God every time there is service? When you die you will be brought at the same alter you are running from anyways, why don't you make it a lifestyle, attending God's house and make it your home. God created everybody but not everyone is the child of God. He is the God of all but not the Father of all. In order to be a child of God you have to be born again. John 3:3 and 1 John 1:7-10 said the blood of Jesus Christ cleanses us from all sins, but we have to confess them in order to be forgiven of them. It is my privilege to introduce you to the Lord Jesus Christ by praying the prayer of salvation found on the next page.

PRAYER OF SALVATION

Lord Jesus Christ I confess all my sins to you, I confess and I believe that you are the Son Of God; you died on the cross for me and rose up on the 3rd day so I can have eternal life. I invite you into my heart and into my life, come rule my life and I surrender all to you. I accept you as my Lord and Savior. I thank you for your Love and for saving me. In Jesus Christ name I pray. Amen

If you have prayed this simple prayer you are now born again or have re-dedicated your life to God, now find a good local church where you are taught the good Word of God and read your Bible daily and pray daily. That is the way you can build your relationship with God and with the Holy Spirit. Let the God of Abraham, Isaac and Israel (Jacob) keep you in perfect peace.

I hope to hear from you, how this book have impacted your life.

ABOUT THE AUTHOR

Archange Malonga is a devoted Christian, great believer in the Word of God and His promises. He takes joy in being used by God for His glory alone, to reach the lost, the broken, and the rejected.

Archange Malonga is anointed with the gift of exhortation and of the spoken Word of God. He is a precious gift in the body of Jesus Christ, whom the saints and the world have yet to discover. He is happily married to his lovely wife Korene and he is a devoted father to his adoring given blessing from God, Elia, Ephraim and Canaan.

www.ingramcontent.com/pod-product-compliance
Lightning Source LLC
Chambersburg PA
CBHW071406090426
42737CB00011B/1376